SEW to SUCCESS!

HOW TO MAKE MONEY IN A HOME-BASED SEWING BUSINESS

An autobiography of
Kathleen Spike,
Professional Dressmaker

Book design -
Linda Wisner

Illustrations -
Kate Pryka

Writing this book was only a dream until Pati Palmer turned it into a reality. Pati and her staff have been a wonderful support system. They provided incredible guidance during the year-long struggle of putting my career story on paper. Pati, I will forever appreciate your belief in my story and my ability to write it.

I owe a special thank you to Susan Pletsch, my editor, for her excellent advice and steady direction. Without her skill, my pages of running manuscript could not have been turned into this book. Her fabulous sense of humor made it **"fun, fast and easy"** - Susan's motto.

Last, but really first, I want to thank my husband Mike. He held me while I cried tears of exhaustion, then cheered me on. He helped me to believe that I could handle the pressures and deadlines of my business and the book. Thanks, Mike, for taking over all of my housework and parenting responsibilities without a complaint. You are the best. Thank you to my son, Shad, and my daughter, Tonya. They have grown up with a fast-moving business and career-minded mom. They have become independent and competent people because of this and I am very proud of them.

Thank you all.

Kathleen Spike

Custom dressmaker Kathleen Spike has turned what is commonly perceived to be a part-time job into a full-time executive-salaried career, all accomplished in her at-home studio.

Kathy learned sewing as a teenager in 4-H, and then turned that love of creating beautiful clothing into a growing business. She has streamlined the concept of custom clothing into a profitable home-based business and credits her college business and marketing classes for starting her on the professional track.

From fabric shop sales to sewing instructor, Kathy has done it all. This includes co-authoring and self-publishing the sewing instruction book **Fast Fashion Jeans For Family Fun**, and founding the Custom Clothing Guild of Oregon (a networking organization of sewing professionals).

A popular speaker with Palmer/Pletsch Associates, Kathy has lectured throughout the United States, in Canada and Australia. She has spoken at the American Home Sewing Association trade show, the American Sewing Guild convention and the "Sewing as a Business" Workshops pilot program in Mississippi. She continues her custom dressmaking business and sewing school, and is an instructor at the Palmer/Pletsch Workshops in Portland, Oregon. A recent challenge for Kathy: She stars in the video version of **Sew to Success**.

Kathy resides in suburban Portland with her husband, Mike Jr., a high school counselor, and their two teenage children, Shad and Tonya.

Table of Contents

My goal in sharing my story is to give you the inspiration, direction and technical business information that will make your home-based sewing business a success. I hope you will laugh along with me when I tell you about my many mistakes, and learn something from them. Through my experience I hope you will gain the courage and knowledge to combine the roles of home-maker, mother and successful business woman.

Kathleen Spike

**Foreword
by Pati Palmer,
President, Palmer/Pletsch Associates**

Custom sewing is growing along with an appreciation for fine hand-made clothing. Kathleen Spike is an excellent role model for the profession. She not only makes an executive salary in her business, but has been a leader for her colleagues. She started the Custom Clothing Guild of Oregon, an organization which enables those sewing for profit to network, upgrade their skills, and ultimately upgrade their income. Most members have tripled their incomes as well as efficiency and quality of their work. We are proud to have Kathleen offer her expertise to you, hoping you may achieve your dream of "having it all — doing what you love, at home, and making money doing it!"

Pati Palmer

CHAPTER 1

My Story

I am a professional dressmaker. I earn $30,000 per year doing work that I love. I began while my children were small and have been at home to watch them grow for all these 17 years. My husband is proud that I am able to contribute substantially to our family income and yet he is delighted that I am able to be at home.

I accomplish a lot because I am willing to work hard. My income is in direct proportion to how much I am willing to sew. You can do as I do. You can earn as much money as you want by deciding how much you want to sew. I am no different from you. I'm a real person who gets tired, has to clean house, hates to pay bills, and loves to sew.

I have, over the last seventeen years, learned some tips, tricks and timesavers that I will share with you. This book is about the growth of my business and it is also a handbook or guide book for you to set up your own business. Are you ready to work hard and make money?

Sewing has been a part of Kathleen's life since she was young. At right she poses with her brothers wearing a pink duster made by her mother. The littlest brother's shorts and jacket were also a "home-made" creation. On page 9 Kathleen (left) models the dress she made for her friend Linda Jones' graduation. At the far right, she wears a beautifully tailored jacket typical of the dressmaking she does today.

I grew up in a rural community in Eastern Oregon where 4-H was a tradition in our family. My three brothers were in 4-H clubs and I was an enthusiastic member of the clothing and cooking club. I was crazy about my sewing, knitting and cooking classes, even way back then! I also had a one-woman cheering section - my MOM!

Throughout grade school and high school Mom and I made all my clothes, from sports things to prom dresses. She has a great sense of color, texture and style. Mom encouraged me to sew what I loved, to be individual, and to follow my fashion instincts.

When I graduated from high school, I won a college scholarship. Most of the girls in my family had gotten married right out of high school, so college was not the usual step. We decided that I would go on to college, but I would have to work to supplement the scholarship. I decided to major in business and marketing, as I thought they would provide me with valuable information and salable skills, no matter what I might do in the future.

I stayed in college for 3½ years until I, too, got married. My husband and I needed my income to help support us while he began his teaching career. Although I have never regretted marrying Mike, I sometimes wish I had finished my last year of college, even though my career now does not require a degree.

Five years later we were the proud parents of a precious baby boy named Shad. Now what to do? This child was such a treasure that I just could not leave him to go back to work. We decided I should be a full-time mother and homemaker, and we would settle for being poor. No two incomes for this family!

When Shad was just three months old, my former employer, who had always admired my wardrobe and sewing abilities, called to ask if I had time to sew some things for her. I was born curious and have always loved a challenge, so I said, "Sure!"

When I completed the wardrobe for her, I instinctively placed a value on my sewing, thanks to my unrelated business experience. When she gave me a check for my work, the light went on!

I realized I had found a second family income and I could stay at home with my baby. Fifteen months after Shad was born our daughter, Tonya, arrived. Now it was definite that I would be an at-home mom. It was clear to me that I would have to work slowly at my new business because of family demands, but I was determined to earn money, to have an interesting career, and to raise our two children.

Kathleen with her family in 1976 - husband Mike and children Shad and Tonya.

CHAPTER 2

Steps to Success

Even back when I sewed that first wardrobe for my former employer, I knew some very important things about myself and my abilities that have helped me to succeed as a dressmaker with a home-based business. I knew that I could sew well. I had won awards in high school and 4-H for my sewing projects and had won compliments on my clothing in the years that followed. I have always had a passion to create beautiful clothes. I was confident I would succeed, even amid the stacks of dirty clothes, fuzz balls in corners and funny green things in my refrigerator.

Working for myself in my home has given me many freedoms:

♦ The ability to accept only the clients and the projects I choose
♦ Freedom from regular office hours
♦ The independence to vary my schedule to accommodate family needs and to avoid boring routine
♦ The elimination of commuting
♦ The ability to spend time with my family during hours other parents are away at work

I have given up:

♦ A built-in social life and easy friendships at the office
♦ The security of a regular paycheck and benefits
♦ A set routine for every day

Personal Traits that Lead to Success

The Cooperative Extension Service booklet "Sewing for Profit" (see page 120) discusses personal traits that lead to success in a home-based custom sewing business. They are:

♦ physical energy	♦ resourcefulness	♦ organizational ability
♦ ambition	♦ nerve - a risk taker	♦ management ability
♦ initiative	♦ tact and diplomacy	♦ self-discipline
♦ self-esteem		

"A home business is not for the procrastinator because there is no one around to make you do your work. Being your own boss may not be easy. Can you schedule time easily? Can you coordinate home, family, and social and work interests with little difficulty? Customers expect work to be done thoroughly and on time. Work that is late or of poor quality because it was done hurriedly will harm your business. Being a good manager, planning a schedule and sticking to it are critical to a successful home business."

Do You Have What it Takes?

Of all of the above, I feel **self-discipline** is one of the most critical to the home-based business person. Are you self-disciplined enough to handle a job where you are the boss and set all the rules and hours? Can you gaze out the window and enjoy the sunshine without closing up shop for the rest of the day? You will have great freedom when you work for yourself, both physically and psychologically. You will also have insecurities if you have been dependent upon a "regular" job with benefits, sick leave, paid vacations, and time clocks.

I am self-disciplined. I make up goals and business plans and put them on paper. A goal or plan in the mind is still a dream. Once committed to paper, goals and plans become real and thus easy to follow. I put my plan on paper and then follow it - it's like a road map that keeps me going in my chosen direction. If I discover my hours are wearing down my health, I change them. If a client is causing a problem, I deal with it immediately. I control my life, it does not control me.

Are you a **risk taker**? The famous French designer Yves St. Laurent says that insecurity is his best friend, because it motivates him to take risks to create his best work. I feel the same way. A person with an empty tummy will work hard to find food, while a person with a full tummy will sit in a chair and snooze. Which are you? Can you financially and emotionally risk never having a guaranteed paycheck? Will you depend on this income to provide food and shelter or will it be used to improve your standard of living? Each will create a different amount of risk.

I am a risk-taker. You'll see several examples of this throughout the book. I like to live on the edge, it keeps me alert to opportunity and learning. But I am a risk-taker with a plan. I plan for an expenditure and then I earn the money. The plan is my motivator.

Can you **withstand pressure** or do you fall apart when the heat is on? To make money it is often not possible to have a client's garment ready days in advance. I may complete a garment minutes before the appointment because I fill my schedule to earn the maximum (though I don't like cutting it quite that close!)

There are **physical requirements** for success in dressmaking. You must have a **strong back** to be able to stand and cut or sit and sew for hours. Standing to cut requires **sturdy legs and feet**, and kneeling to fit requires **good knees**. I found I was allergic to certain Harris Tweeds or to the finish on these fabrics. Every time I worked on this hand-loomed tweed I suffered severe congestion. This doesn't affect my working as a dressmaker, but it does eliminate that fabric from my list. Do you have any fabric allergies that you know of?

Check Your Skills

Basic sewing skills you should have before sewing for profit:
- ☐ Understanding measuring and choosing best commercial pattern size
- ☐ Training or experience fitting problem figures
- ☐ Experience sewing on many different fabrics
- ☐ Awareness of and experience in using new products and sewing techniques: fusible interfacings, sewing with knits, synthetic leather and suedes such as Ultrasuede,® rainwear fabrics, Lycra® stretch fabrics
- ☐ Experience in sewing a variety of garment types: dresses, skirts, blouses, shirts, pants, jackets, blazers, coats, suits, and both casual and evening wear

Skills to Master in the Future

- ◆ Quality speed sewing techniques
- ◆ Pattern drafting
- ◆ Draping
- ◆ Basic sloper fitting and designing from a sloper
- ◆ Classic tailoring
- ◆ Wardrobe planning
- ◆ Sewing fur and leather

- ◆ Figure flattery through appropriate design selection
- ◆ Clothing embellishment
- ◆ Color analysis
- ◆ Fashion illustration, history of fashion
- ◆ Textile production
- ◆ Psychology, communications, public speaking

Practice by sewing for friends and family!

CHAPTER 3

Success Stories

My love of people and family, of being at home, of sewing and fashion, blended with a love of beautiful fabrics created my career as a dressmaker.

At this stage in my professional career, I choose the projects and the clients I want to work with. I prefer fine fabrics and my prices are high to discourage my clients from putting my time in on anything but the best. I have narrowed my clientele to those who appreciate fine craftsmanship and are prepared to pay me for my experience.

I like to work on a complete wardrobe with a client, sewing all the garments that she chooses to have made. I have focused on tailored jackets and coats and have developed a strong business and good reputation for fitting and sewing pants. I also sew dresses, blouses, sportswear and special occasion clothing.

I make my money from the volume of sewing I'm able to do. I can have 25 garments cut and in stages of fitting, another 20 in various stages of construction, and at least 25 pieces being preshrunk or waiting to be cut. My lead time is six to eight weeks. I have learned to schedule myself so that this number is not overwhelming to me, just business as usual.

I think my favorite part of the business is being an ongoing part of my client's lives. We work together creating a beautifully-dressed image that is unique. I am as much a part of their successes as they are of mine.

I'm a "success story" in dressmaking, but my story isn't the only one. Here are more success stories - all professional acquaintances in the Portland, Oregon area. Each woman has a unique business and a special set of circumstances that work for her. I hope they will inspire you to think beyond traditional dressmaking for your career. (See page 120 if you would like to contact any of them.)

Delores Diane Kelley, Custom Interior Sewing

Delores Kelley has always loved sewing but only dreamed of being paid for her work. After her children were grown, she began experimenting in the area of sewing businesses. Finding that dressmaking wasn't for her because she was uncomfortable with garment fitting, she went on to dress windows, sofas and beds instead!

Delores went to work for a small custom interior workroom, learning all she could about the business and the products she was creating. When her employer decided to sell, Delores was ready to buy. She has been in the field for seven years and a business owner for a year and a half.

She works with interior designers and decorators producing fabulous custom curtains, draperies, window shades, dust ruffles, bedspreads, pillows, bedroom and bathroom accessories. A peek into Delores' workroom before an order is picked up is like looking at the latest home decorating magazines. The colors and fabrics are exciting and always changing, as this is also a fashion business. Gorgeous chintz fabrics, great balloon shades and enormous draperies crowd her work area.

During her training Delores learned to fabricate (to see a picture and create what she saw), estimate yardage, match pattern repeats, arrange pleats so seams don't show, and use all of the formulas in the decorating industry. One of her most important tasks is communicating with interior designers.

"Designers often have an idea but cannot translate it to paper or even put it into exact words. My job is to be skilled and experienced enough to understand their final goal and to be able to make it come to life," says Delores.

This type of home-based sewing business requires space to produce and store bulky products and to house industrial equipment. Delores uses a padded 60" × 108" work table, a blind hemmer machine (to hem yards and yards of fabric!), a serger, a standard zigzag machine, and a good steam iron. She cuts by hand, often single layer because of matching repeating prints.

Delores is a very organized person and is accustomed to precision work. Drapes must hang perfectly straight, with square corners. This requires attention to detail. She uses a unique system of sturdy racks hung from the ceiling to hang draperies and other window coverings, both while she is working on them (to check the hang of the fabric and for holding the work while hemming) and for storage until they are picked up. The function of this rack system is somewhat like that of a dress form that allows the dressmaker to stand back and view her work.

Her organization and precision extend to the business area. A neat and tidy desk holds many special forms and systems Delores has developed to streamline her work. For example, she created a sophisticated color-coded system for orders coming in, orders in progress, and orders to be picked up that helps her easily keep track of the status of each piece.

Delores has a price list for each item and each variation of the basic piece. Interior designers use this price list to help them give estimates to the client. Delores feels she earns an average of $7 per hour, working part time, and generates approximately $11,000 per year. She works at her own pace and as hard as she chooses. She has little problem with outstanding invoices or slow payments. Designers pay her in a timely fashion because they want her to do more work for them.

If you are interested in this style of home-based sewing business, Delores suggests you seek an apprenticeship as she did, be creative, love color and fabric, and enjoy the finished product. It is important to have a mind for detail, patience, math aptitude (she constantly uses her calculator), self-confidence and self-motivation.

Paula D. Marineau,
Wearable Art Designer

While her children were growing, Paula became what she calls "a sewing class junkie" — taking every class she could find! Years of sewing experience took a new direction when she took a quilting class. Her first project was a handbag that a friend loved. Paula made one for her and has now made hundreds.

Another friend said, "Paula, if you can make this handbag, why can't you make a quilted coat?" A coat was created. Paula's friends thought it was so beautiful they convinced her to show it in a wearable art fashion show. That coat sold for $600. Now her coats sell for $1300.

The business now consists of creating wearable art garments, particularly pieced coats and jackets. Her focus is on piping, binding, tucking, pleating - influences from clothing from the 1930's to 1950's. Her wearable art is just that, wearable rather than museum pieces. Cotton is a favorite fabric, but silks, wools and polyesters are used as well.

Paula's customer is the individual who is looking for something unique. Paula works for several months creating 10 to 15 special designs. She then sends invitations to a sale held in her beautiful home studio.

In addition to her sale, Paula designs custom garments. The client may choose colors, but Paula has the final say in how she will use the different fabrics. This is where the artist takes over. She does all of her own cutting, feeling this is where she makes or breaks a garment. She has two wonderful dressmakers who assist her in construction.

The only items needed to start this kind of business are a sewing machine and storage for fabrics and scraps. Paula's sewing machine is 29 years old. Since most of the work is finished by covering the edges with fabric, she feels a serger is not a requirement, but uses hers on some pieces.

"You need to be a 'gatherer' to be in this business," says Paula. "A collector of fabrics. You must learn to create something from nothing." She suggests keeping fabric in clear storage boxes to see what you have, which is the inspiration to create.

Paula regularly goes through the wastebaskets after a day of work to make sure a valuable scrap isn't accidentally tossed. Because she does "pieced" clothing, even the smallest piece has artistic value.

Paula feels she has not yet mastered pricing. She prices by artistic instinct and thinks she has a good feel about what her market will bear. It doesn't matter if the fabric cost only $1.00 per yard, it is what she has done with it that creates the value. When working part-time and alone, Paula generated about $10,000 annually. She feels if she worked full-time with her two employees she could earn up to $50,000 per year.

Paula works for self-fulfillment, not for survival. Her husband is very supportive. A craftsperson too, he builds museum-quality model ships and airplanes. He goes to his work area at 7 pm, saying "I'll meet you for the news at 10." He is delighted Paula has her business, so she isn't upset when he heads for the basement.

Paula's advice to anyone wanting this type of home-based business is to know technical skill but not be a technical perfectionist, as it kills creativity. Have a personality that can break from the rules. Learn to go with creative instincts and to take financial risk, as you must invest in fabrics before getting paid for a product. A good sense of color is a necessity too.

Paula has created a business that wants to grow; she is just deciding how much. From my viewpoint, the sky is the limit for Paula if she wants to take the flight.

Jeanne Scolaro Brown, Designer Sample Maker

Jeanne is a sample maker in a home-based business. Jeanne's love for sewing developed out of necessity. As one of five children she learned at an early age to take responsibility for sewing her own clothing. She loved it! She expanded this love for sewing and fabric by working in a very special fabric shop during high school. While attending college, Jeanne worked in garment factories during vacations. She feels her best education was this on-the-job experience.

One job was in a bedspread factory. She was introduced to and trained in a variety of specific industrial machines. This was to become the major training ground for her present business. She feels it would be difficult to have developed her home-based business without industry connections and experience.

Jeanne feels her best training for sample making was with Nike in Beaverton, Oregon. She established her strongest connections with pattern-makers there, and learned what was expected of a sample maker.

Jeanne started her home-based business when she and her husband adopted their daughter and she wanted to be at home full-time. She tried dressmaking, but found the attention, education and conversation required with the client to be too stressful. She turned to sample making (a solitary task) which provided her with more hours of production as compared to hours of conversation with clients.

Jeanne suggests having a straight stitch and cover stitch power machine with a ½ horsepower motor. Used ones are available. You can use a home sewing machine but it is not as fast so it eats up valuable production time. Because it is not a heavy duty machine, it is easy to burn out a motor.

Jeanne's prices vary with the customer. If she likes working with a client, she will be flexible in price while the client works her way up. The industry is a tough one, and Jeanne helps her customers to succeed so she can succeed. She will survive and grow only if they do. Jeanne keeps careful track of all time spent on every sample. If she is underpaid or overpaid, she will tell the customer so that the next time the price will be adjusted. She takes risks and will try any project once. Jeanne says, "I'm good at what I do and designers are usually willing to pay my price."

Jeanne works primarily with the patternmaker who is working for the designer or company. At times the patternmaker becomes the designer and the sample maker becomes the patternmaker, because each person must know how to sew the garment most efficiently, how it fits, and the look of the final product. If the patternmaker knows the entire sewing process, many problems are worked out before the garment arrives at the sample maker. The more experience the designer and the patternmaker have, the less input they need from Jeanne. She is allowed more creativity if they need her experience.

The sample maker is at the bottom of the prestige chain. Jeanne is thinking about moving up into designing, still in a home-based setting. Her daughter is getting older and goes to school part-time so Jeanne has more potential business time.

Working part-time and running her home as a traditional mother, Jeanne feels she earns about $8,000 per year at an hourly rate of $10 to $12. "If I were to be the major breadwinner, I would have to work full-time, duplicate myself by hiring employees, and go into light manufacturing. There is a lot of money to be made in light manufacturing if you can stand the non-stop diet of doing the same thing over and over again," says Jeanne.

Jeanne feels she owes part of her success to being forceful, hard-working and cooperative, and not being afraid to verbalize her ideas and business needs. Her advice is to make connections in the industry through working and networking.

Ann Franzen,
Garment Manufacturer

Ann Franzen owns a clothing manufacturing business located in her home. Her business is mass producing any type of garment. Ann has never formally advertised; happy customers refer others to her and business just keeps marching in the door.

Ann was not always involved in sewing. Previously, she owned a retail dance and aerobic wear store. When customers began to ask for custom merchandise, she saw an opportunity to increase profits, fill non-productive store hours, and increase customer good will. She developed a custom aerobic wear and costume business that she enjoyed so much, she decided to do it full-time. She also moved the entire operation home, so she could be with her toddlers all the time. She also realized a jump in profits.

Being another self-taught professional, Ann developed her expertise through taking classes, studying books and building a good reference library, investigating retail garments, viewing exhibits of costumes and historical clothing. She is ingenious, creative and determined - three major assets to her business.

Having tried every facet of sewing-for-profit (tailoring, dressmaking, costuming, bridal, and more), Ann has settled on light manufacturing. It gives her mind the chance to be free and spin dreams of family and business as she zooms through stacks of uniforms. She says, "After sewing one garment fifty times, I see more ways to do it to cut time and improve profits." Ann's goal is to develop her business to a point where she is managing seamstresses who will produce all of her goods, and she will return to sewing for pleasure.

Ann operates on contracts. She studies a potential project, decides what she wants to make per hour plus overhead, and gives a bid. The customer can accept, reject, or negotiate her bid.

Ann says she could not completely support herself and her family right now. If she were working full-time she could survive. Her goal is to make less per hour but have many more accounts and help with the work: $5 per hour × 10 accounts = $50 per hour, where $10.00 × 1 account = $10 per hour. This is the same formula the garment industry uses. Her per-hour charge at this time is $10 to $12, and her yearly salary is approximately $15,000.

Mass production of clothing requires an industrial power sewing machine. It is faster and stronger for the extended hours it will be in use. Ann feels the power machine also has a stronger stitch. The few garments that are returned to her for repairs are those that were sewn on a home sewing machine. Power machines are quite large, though, so you will need more space.

Other tools needed would be a large (6′ × 8′ if possible) cutting table as you will be working with yards and yards of fabric. A commercial power fabric saw (which can cut 8″ of fabric at a time) or a commercial rotary cutter (which will cut ¾″ deep layers of fabric) are important if you plan to be in real production. If cutting by hand, four thicknesses are the maximum you can cut. That dramatically affects profits.

You will need an area and a system for labeling and storing the cut pieces. They must be carefully categorized by piece, size and color. Mixing them up can take hours to sort out, and that means lost profits.

Ann uses private contractors at times to help her with the work load. Her husband, Mike, is her new cutter. "We are keeping all of the profits in the family. It creates some stress though, as he wants to be 'the boss'! He is thinking about being in charge and keeping the profits — Is this corporate raiding?" Ann laughs!

To run your own business at home, Ann feels you must be able to enjoy being alone, be self-disciplined, and be willing to work long hours. Ann's best advice is to stand behind any work that you do, no matter what the cost. Do not be embarrassed by returned work, just fix it. A satisfied customer is the best good will any business can have.

CHAPTER 4

Starting Your Business - What to Do First

Good Advice Publications

Set up your business as professionally as possible. Call the Small Business Administration and get their advice. Read their two publications, **Thinking About Going Into Business** (MA2.025) and **Checklist For Going Into Business** (MA2.016). They also have a booklet that lists all free publications (Pub. 115-A). See page 120 for ordering information. These may help you decide if you fit the criteria for being a business owner. Once you have made your choice to launch your business, use the following steps and my checklist on page 40 to chart your progress.

Permits and Licenses

First, apply for a business license. This is how our cities keep track of all businesses, regardless of size. Call your town administrator, city hall, or county and ask what the requirements are for a business license for a home-based business. You may or may not need one in your locality. In Gresham, Oregon, my home, the fee for a business license is $25. It differs in other areas.

When you have been granted your license, frame it and post it in your studio. It helps to create a professional atmosphere and gives your clients confidence in the legitimacy of your business. My business license looks like this:

POST IN A CONSPICUOUS PLACE

LICE

EXPIRAT

This license evidences payment of the fee required by the Gresham Code 8.015 and shall not be construed as authorizing conduct in violation of any law.

LICENSE T

BUSINESS

BUSINESS ADDRESS: 1880 SW HEINEY RD

OWNER / OFFICER: KATHLEEN SPIKE

TO   GARMENT CLASSICS
1880 SW HEINEY RD
GRESHAM OR 97030-0000

TOTA

CITY OF GRESHAM LICENS

23

In my city, I also have to fill out an **Application for Home Occupation Permit**. You can see from this form that my community is working to protect the quality of life in its residential neighborhoods. I'm glad! Many communities welcome home-based businesses, as often they are the only homes occupied during working hours - a safety factor for the neighborhood.

City of Gresham
1333 N W EASTMAN AVENUE
GRESHAM, OREGON 97030

APPLICATION
HOME OCCUPATION PERMIT

If you operate your business from your residence within the City limits of Gresham, you must complete all applicable information below and submit it with your business license application to the Cashier.

Date_____ Business Name_____

Applicant Name_____ License No._____

Address_____ File Date _____

City_____ State_____ Zip_____ Date Aprv._____

Owner____ Renter____ Home Phone_____ Renew Date_____

Property Owner's Name and Address_____
_____

Describe your business activity and service or goods to be provided or manufactured.(Please Be Specific)_____
_____
_____
_____

What part(s) of the activities occur at the residence?_____
_____
_____
_____

The issuance of a Gresham Business License is not a permit to conduct a Home Occupation. The issuance of A Home Occupation is contingent upon the acceptance of this application and continued compliance with the provisions of Section 4.0620 of the Community Development Standards listed on the reverse side.

The Home Occupation permit will be valid for a two year period and must be renewed. Noncompliance with any of the provisions listed below will result in revocation of the Permit, as provided by Section 4.0680.

A. No sign is to be used.

B. There is no display that will indicate from the exterior that the building is used in whole or in part for any purpose other than a dwelling.

C. The building retains the characteristics of a residence and no more than 25% of the gross floor area is used for the business.

D. There is no outside storage of materials other than plant material intended as landscaping.

E. There are no employees at the home other than family members who reside at the dwelling.

F. The use will not tend to destroy the residential character of the neighborhood.

G. The generation of any noise, vibrations,odors, heat or glare detectable beyond any property line is prohibited.

I have read the above requirements and I agree to comply with the aforementioned standards established for a Home Occupation Permit.

_____ _____
Property Owner's Signature   Applicant's Signature

Date_____ Date_____

Some states require a "stuffed items" license. Submit a sample of the stuffing (for pillows, toys, etc.) for approval and obtain a label indicating content. Flammability is another area that is regulated in some states. Contact your local Cooperative Extension Service for information. My state Textiles and Clothing Specialist sent me the chart on the next page.

Trade Names and Business Names

If you use a business name (mine has been Garment Classics, I just changed to KS Designs), your county or state may require you to fill out a DBA (Doing Business As) card. Its purpose is to prevent anyone else from using your business name, and it is kept on file in case anyone should have a business complaint against you. I obtained my DBA application from my bank. Registration of trademarks and tradenames is a separate process and fee - you may need a lawyer's help.

Sales Tax

Most states have sales tax and often there are city and county taxes too. If you make anything for sale or buy goods for resale, you must apply for a sales authorization certificate. This document has a resale tax number that will enable you to buy, without paying sales tax, any materials at wholesale price for resale.

If you have sales tax, you are responsible for collecting this tax from each client at the time of delivery, keeping accurate records, then paying your tax agency. You can factor that tax percentage into your cost per hour, or add it to the end of every bill. If you fail to do this, at the end of the tax period the tax authorities may hand you a bill so large it would put you out of business. (see page 73)

Sales tax information and application forms may be obtained from your State Department of Taxation and Finance, Sales Tax Bureau.

Zoning

Zoning regulations vary from city to city. A home-based business is a business in a residential setting and there are often restrictions on this. Size of sign, amount of noise, volume of traffic and outside structures are often regulated. Again, this is done as a protection to keep neighborhoods safe and happy for residents. See my "Application for Home Occupation Permit" for some specific examples of these protective measures. Even though I am legally operating within my home, I check with my neighbors to make sure the cars that are arriving are not causing them any inconvenience.

State of Oregon Custom Sewing Business License/Regulations

License/Registration	Cost/Source	Comments
Registration of Business Name Applies to business operating under fictitious name rather than the owner's. Protects business name in each county registered. Protects customers in learning the ownership of a business in cases of liability.	$10 plus $2 for each county for 2 yrs. State of Oregon Department of Commerce Corporation Division 158 12th Street N.E. Salem, OR 97310 (503) 378-4166	If business name is own full legal name, i.e., **Draperies by Jane Doe**, no need to register. For a fictitious or incomplete name, i.e. **Jane's Draperies**, registration is required.
Registration of Trademark (or Tradename) - Protects mark or name and records ownership.	$10 for 5 years State of Oregon Dept. of Commerce (above)	
Local Business License - To regulate businesses in a given location and produce income for the licensing agency	Cost varies City Hall of city in which business is located.	Check with your city office. Not all cities require a license.
Federal ID Number (Form SS-4) - Registers you with IRS, Social Security Administration and Department of Labor.	No fee Call nearest Internal Revenue office for forms.	Required for any new business.
Zoning - Check if location is business zoned. Avoids unnecessary disturbance from business in residential area.	Contact local city or county planning department.	Zoning generally not a limitation unless business has heavy traffic or other disturbance.
Stuffed Items (stuffed toys, upholstered furniture)	No Oregon State regulations. For copy of federal regulations call Consumer Product Safety Commission, Washington, D.C., 1-800-638-2772.	
Stuffed Items (pillows and bedding)	No Oregon State regulations. For copy of federal regulations call Federal Trade Commission, Washington, D.C., (202) 523-3598.	

IF YOU BECOME AN EMPLOYER OF OTHER PERSONS:

Combined Employer's Registration Report	Oregon Department of Revenue P.O. Box 14800 Salem, OR 97310	You'll receive booklet: "Information for Oregon Employers" and blank forms for payroll taxes.
Workers' Compensation Insurance Registration - Protection for all employees.	Required for all employers. Three choices include: 1) Oregon State Accident Insurance Fund (SAIF) 2) private insurance carrier 3) self-insured as required by Workers' Compensation Dept., Salem, OR 378-3413.	
Employee's Withholding Exemption Certificate (W-4 forms)	U.S. Treasury Department Internal Revenue Service	A form is required for each employee hired.

Courtesy of Ardis Koester, Ph.D., Extension Textiles and Clothing Specialist, Oregon State University, Corvallis, Oregon

CHAPTER 5

Create a Successful Business

I began my business not realizing that I was, in fact, starting a business. Many of you may have done the same. **Now** I have a formal business plan that helps me grow in an orderly fashion.

Because a custom dressmaking business can begin with very little investment and grow with self-financing instead of a bank loan, a formal plan is not always as important in the beginning as with other businesses. However, a business plan helps you to answer important questions.

A favorite reference book, **Women Working Home**, (see page 121), describes a business plan as follows:

A business plan is written to:
1. Establish what your business objectives are and indicate how you will reach them.
2. Help you discover, in advance, areas where problems may occur.
3. Indicate to your banker exactly how the borrowed monies will be spent and where the profits will be made to further the company's goals and to reward the investor.

Begin a Business Plan

Women Working Home presents the following questions to be answered before a real business plan can be created. I have paraphrased the ones I feel are pertinent to a sewing business. Ponder and answer the following questions and you'll have the beginnings of a business plan. For precisely how to write a business plan, see **Women Working Home** for an easy-to-follow format.

♦ **What business am I in?** Deciding exactly what your business will be and focusing all your energy in one spot will help you to progress faster.

♦ **What product or service am I selling?** Define your service or product in detail. Will you be sewing women's clothing or bridal?

♦ **Who is my competition?** Knowing your competition helps to decide what to sell, for how much, to whom, and even what hours to keep.

♦ **Why am I developing a business?** People generally build businesses for reasons based on personal needs and financial expectations.

♦ **How much money is needed to operate this business?** List your start-up costs (equipment, home remodeling, insurance, telephone, licenses and permits, beginning advertising, etc.). Project business expenses for each month and create a rock-bottom, bare-bones budget. A budget can help you visualize cash flow - where money comes from and where it goes.

> NOTE: If you have start-up costs, plan where you will get the money. Can you borrow from the family budget, borrow from a relative, have a garage sale?

♦ **Who are my customers and where are they located?** Discovering what potential customers' desires are, then satisfying their wants and needs with your product or service can bring them to your door, provided they see or hear about your product.

♦ **How much time am I willing to devote to a business?** It is important to schedule working hours. Set daily or weekly objectives: "I am going to work five hours a day, 9am-12pm and 1-3pm." Or, "I am going to work 25 hours per week." Ask your family to help you establish a workable time schedule. Involving them often helps bring sympathy and understanding for your busy schedule.

Find Your Best Business Niche

In talking about business plans I asked you to think about the most important questions:
♦ What business am I in?
♦ What product or service am I selling?
♦ Who is my customer?

This, in a nutshell, is marketing. Often new businesses try to sell the greatest number of products to the widest audience, when the key is to narrow your focus. Nothing kills a business faster than trying to sell the wrong product to the wrong audience. It doesn't matter that you **LOVE** to sew tennis clothes if no one in your area plays tennis. Successful marketing is aiming the right product or service toward the right market. Successful marketing comes from:

1. Researching, analyzing, and evaluating your potential customers.
2. Efficiently producing salable products or services.
3. Communicating your products or services to your customers.

Study Yourself

It is important to know yourself well. Ask yourself these questions:

♦ What knowledge or skills do you have that others need or want?
♦ What experiences do you have to offer others?
♦ What tangible results or benefits do your products or services produce for your potential customer? Your customer will subconsciously be asking "What's in this for me?"
♦ What are your strengths; what do you do best?
♦ What are your weaknesses; what do you not do well?

Answers here should help you create a product or service that is something you are good at and something you want to do.

Study Your Potential Product or Service

♦ Do you like working with people, or do you prefer little or no client contact?
♦ How are your fitting skills? Will you be able to deal with many different shapes and sizes of bodies? Is there someplace you can go to study fitting?
♦ How much work space do you have available? Some products, draperies and home decorating for example, require large spaces to produce large products.
♦ Do you need variety and excitement in your work, or are you content to continually produce the same product or service?
♦ Do you have a need to constantly be creative or are you comfortable executing someone else's creativity?

NOTE: See my chapters "Success Stories" page 14 and "Specializing Can Mean Greater Profit" page 59 for more information on the many different possibilities for a home-based sewing business.

Study Your Potential Sewing Business Market

♦ Who are your potential customers?
♦ How many different types of potential customers do you have?
♦ What benefits are they looking for?
♦ Where are they located?
♦ What is their income level?
♦ What price will they pay for your product?
♦ How can you reach them?
♦ Are their needs already being met by an existing business?

The above questions should help you decide exactly what product or service you will be happiest producing, and to whom you will sell.

Make a Plan

Set down realistic objectives for yourself and your business. Be specific about both money and time. Then create ways to achieve your goals. If you want to sew scarves and you want to earn $100 per week, and you think you can sell your scarves for $10 each, you will have to schedule to sew 10 scarves. If it takes you four hours per scarf, that equals a 40-hour week, and you have not allowed time for purchasing materials nor for selling your product. Perhaps you should re-evaluate your plan, as that is a lot of work and many hours for less than minimum wage.

	Scarf A	Scarf B
Want to earn	$100	$100
Can sell product for	$10*	$12*
Must produce	10	8
Time to produce each	4 hours	3 hours
Time spent each week	40 hours	24 hours
Earn per hour	$2.50	$4.16

*Plus materials cost

Put Your Plan Into Action

Good planning is important, but it requires action to make something happen. Create deadlines for yourself and mark them on your calendar.

May 1   Have all my business licenses and permits in order.

May 20   I will have spoken to my accountant and insurance agent and will have a plan for these areas.

May 30   Have sewing space organized so that on June 1, I can begin to sew my product.

June 1   Begin producing scarves in my organized space and I will produce them so efficiently that it will take three hours or less.

Allow ample time to put your marketing plan into action and be flexible if you miss a deadline. You are new at this but you are learning fast!

*This is one of my satisfied clients modeling her
fabulous new winter coat that we created together.*

CHAPTER 6

Think, Look, and Act Like a Business

♦ Set your own priorities and those of your family. Plan quality time for everyone, including yourself.

♦ Create a separate place for your business. Minimize distraction so you can concentrate on your work. Close the door or put up a "Do Not Disturb" sign if you need to.

♦ Match changing energy to the task. Some things require your best time of day, some don't. I cut in the morning when I am fresh because this requires concentration, and hem, a lower energy task, in the evening.

♦ Set definite work hours. Schedule a regular housework routine that will not interfere with your office/studio hours. I do house chores before and after working hours because I like to work in uninterrupted blocks of time.

♦ Arrange your work space so the items you use most are within easy reach. Replace them after use so you won't waste valuable time. Time is money!

♦ Have a separate telephone line with an answering machine and record a business-like message.

♦ Stay out of the refrigerator!

♦ Treat household interruptions as if you were at an office. Learn to say nicely but firmly, "No, I'm working now."

♦ Get out of the house each day, even to take a walk. Don't let yourself become isolated from the human race.

♦ Dress for work: shower, do your hair, put on your face, wear suitable attractive clothing and, if it is your style, earrings. Be attractively dressed for your family, your clients, and to create a "successful person" attitude for yourself.

1. Snacking
2. Sleeping late
3. Procrastinating
4. Talking on the phone
5. Watching TV
6. Getting sloppy, staying in nightclothes all day
7. Taking too long to read the newspaper
8. Drinking while working
9. Spending too much time visiting neighbors
10. Working too much.

Working From Home

Set Up an Efficient Business Office

I constantly use the following supplies and think you will too.

♦ **File folders** - Each client has her own file containing her measurement chart (the "Lady"), copies of her work orders that are swatched so I have an accurate record of what I have sewn for her, and any other information pertaining to that individual. (See Client Records, page 77.)

♦ **File drawer or box** - I now have real file cabinets, but for years I used a cardboard file drawer that was just fine. I store client files alphabetically; then other information by subject. Mail-order notions catalogs, fabric color cards, magazine fashion "inspiration" clippings, and much more are carefully filed away.

♦ **Standard office supplies** - I have duplicates for my family so my business supplies are ready for me when I need them:

paper clips	eraser
stapler and staples	pens
paper punch	soft tip pens
Scotch® tape	postal scale
paper scissors	postage stamps
pencils	telephone message pads
pencil sharpener	note pads

♦ **Business bill-paying equipment** - Business checkbook, envelopes, business return address labels.

♦ **Bookkeeping supply** - Record sheets, files and envelopes.

♦ **Calculator with a tape** (My accountant insisted!) - Make sure the tape is standard paper, not thermal paper, which fades in the light. Your records will disappear!

♦ **Pen and pencil holder** - Placed where my clients have easy access, so check-writing is convenient for them.

Business Cards and Stationery

One of the first things that helped me *feel* like a business was getting my first business cards. Other people respond positively to cards too. I think this is an important step to take early in your business planning. Cards can be used for:

1. **Advertising** - Call on fabric shops with samples of your work; leave a quantity of cards for referrals.

2. **Advertising again** - Post your card on your grocery store or other bulletin boards if they reach your target customers.

3. **Word of mouth advertising** - Give extra cards to your clients (the best and cheapest exposure).

4. **Appointment cards** (like the dentist).

Business cards validate the authenticity of even a brand-new business.

Printed stationery is another form of business printing that you may want to consider. All business correspondence should be written on business paper. Remember this is advertising too, as your business name will be printed on both the paper and envelope. This all adds to your professional image. I find I use half-sheets (5½" × 8") and small envelopes more than I do full sheets and letter-size envelopes. I write more business notes than full-page letters.

Business stationery adds a touch of importance to everything you write, even your daily to-do list! I send my children's notes to school on business stationery because it is more professional and faster - My name, address and phone number are already there.

You can find some great bargains in printed products for your first step. The sky is the limit at the other end. The ultimate is to have a custom logo designed by a graphic artist and printed on cards, stationery, and garment labels. This is what I am doing now, after all these years in business. This sizable investment fits with the continued growth and upgrading of my business. I began with the most basic items produced very inexpensively. See how my business cards have improved with my business:

My new cards have a shiny red background with white type, and I love my choice.

Your business paper goods should include the following information:

◆ Name, address, phone number (including area code)

◆ What you do — Custom Dressmaking, Alterations, etc.

◆ Your specialty if you have one - for example, custom dressmaking, bridal gowns.

◆ Your hours of business, including days you work if limited.

Some people are uncomfortable using their home address for privacy reasons. You may use only your phone number if you choose. I use my address because I want all of my information in one place. You can rent a post office box to avoid using your home address, but that is an added expense; and then you must go to the post office every day.

Here are some places to contact for inexpensive paper goods:

Call local quick printers. They do stock business cards in my area for about $20 for 500. Prices vary so call around for the best price. You can generally choose from white or colored paper with black ink as standard. You may also select a stock logo from a book of possibilities. You may find stock designs of a needle and thread, a thread spool, a dress form. Choose one that represents what you do and that is in good taste.

Mail-order catalogs:

Walter Drake 69 Drake Building Colorado Springs, CO 80940	Has very inexpensive ($2.98 for 200) business cards, very inexpensive stationery, mailing labels, return address labels, garment labels. Write for a catalog.
Amsterdam Printing and Litho Corp. Wallins Corners Rd. Amsterdam, NY 12010-1899 1-800-833-6231	They make all types of business forms, mailing labels, etc. Call for a catalog.
The Stationery House 1000 Florida Avenue Hagerstown, MD 21741 1-800-638-3033	Inexpensive business cards and other paper goods. Write for a catalog.
Nebs 500 Maine Street Gorton, MA 01471 1-800-225-6380	Business forms, mailing labels, every type of printed form you can imagine. Write for a catalog.

Watch out for large minimum orders or large quantities. Throwing away a large inventory of outdated paper if you change your specialty or move is costly. The lowest prices are for large quantities, but sometimes that is a false savings. Order minimum quantities for your first order. You can always make changes without guilt when you have to reprint because you ran out!

Garment Labels

Another good image maker is a sew-in fabric label for the garments or items you create. This is also advertising — every time your satisfied client slips on her new dress she sees your name. Ready-to-wear manufacturers spend a lot of money on quality labels for a reason — it brings them repeat customers.

Labels can be quite reasonable for stock designs and very costly for a custom product. My labels have changed over the years. They are shown here at half size.

The first label is a woven fabric with a printed message, the others are woven labels with the message woven in as well. All-woven is considerably more expensive and luxurious. I was perfectly happy with my first labels; but as the quality of my work improved, I wanted my labels to reflect that fact.

Here are some good sources for labels:

Northwest Tag and Label 110 Foothills Road Lake Oswego, OR 97034	Quality custom-printed labels with prices beginning at $24.50 for 250 labels. Look for their ads in sewing publications or write for information.
Charm Woven Labels Box 30027 Portland, OR 97230	This company also advertises in sewing publications. Prices range from $3.25 for 12 labels to $37 for 500.
Heirloom Woven Labels Grand Central Post Office PO Box 2188 New York, NY 10163	An all-woven label that is surprisingly inexpensive for the quality. Write for a color brochure. Prices range from $18.50 for 36, to $34.50 for 144 labels.
Alkahn Woven Labels 0108 S.W. Thomas Portland, OR 97201	An expensive and luxurious woven label available in unlimited custom designs, the "ultimate label."

NOTE: There may be an initial artwork charge in addition to prices quoted.

Talk to a Tax Specialist

When I first started my business, I was concerned about keeping good financial records. I talked to several accountants who intimidated and frustrated me with the "Little Lady" routine: "Little Lady, don't you worry about those things. Just stay at home with your family." Well! Here I was, doing my best to establish myself as a business (even though my income was just $2000 that first year) and that was the response!

Thank goodness I finally met a young accountant who felt as I did - that I had a growing business and should be starting in a professional and responsible manner. He advised my husband and me on my business as it related to family tax matters, and on setting up my business books.

Now I go to the accountant only once a year for tax preparation. The accountant set up such a simple bookkeeping system that I do my own book work all year. But I must confess, my bookkeeping is so straightforward that I taught my daughter Tonya how to do my books when she was just 13 years old. She still, at age 16, posts all of my income and expenses, makes my deposits, and balances my business checkbook. (See page 69 for my bookkeeping system.)

Why You Need Tax Advice Now

Times have changed enough since I began my business 17 years ago that you should not get the reaction from accountants that I did. This is important because one of the most critical steps you can take is to start your business off on the right foot with good record-keeping and tax advice. Make an appointment with a tax specialist for these two important steps:

1. Get advice on how your estimated income for one year will affect your family's tax planning. Wouldn't it be dreadful to earn and spend $10,000, only to find out you owed $3000 in taxes - and your money is gone. By planning ahead and knowing what can potentially happen, you can set aside money to pay taxes, or you can pay "Estimated Quarterly Taxes" to avoid surprises April 15.

2. Get help in setting up simple records so you can easily keep track of income and expenses. You should also learn what items are deductible, and how to save and store receipts to prove expenses. (See page 68 for more on record-keeping.)

Who to See

Tax and record-keeping specialists include:

♦ **Certified Public Accountants (CPA):** $50-$100 per hour. The most expensive and most learned advice you can get. Consider making an appointment for one hour (include your spouse) to discuss tax implications of your additional earnings, then request a referral to a good bookkeeper for less costly record-keeping advice.

♦ **Accountants:** $38-$60 per hour. These professionals are trained in tax work but have not taken (or passed) the CPA exam. I would suggest you treat them as you would a CPA and buy one hour to discuss major tax work, then ask for a referral for record-keeping.

♦ **Tax consultants:** $35-$50 per hour. They are perhaps the most knowledgeable about tax issues because it is all they do, while a CPA or accountant is involved in many aspects of a business, beyond taxes.

♦ **Full charge bookkeepers:** $12-$25 per hour. These specialists are the best for record-keeping instruction because record-keeping is their primary function. One of the above specialists may get too complex for a new small business, but good bookkeepers understand that "simple is best." Often we get the most for our money here. "Full charge" indicates they are familiar with year end statements and tax records, and can give you advice about business deductions. They are not the best, however, for overall family tax strategy.

Many of these tax specialists are full service firms - they may have all four categories of specialists at various hourly rates in one office, plus computer capabilities for processing your records and preparing tax work.

How to Find Someone With Whom You Are Comfortable

The best way to find a tax specialist who has the right skills for you is to ask friends in similar financial positions and businesses for referrals. You can also look in the Yellow Pages under "Tax."

Ask to schedule an interview at no charge at which you and the tax specialist can decide if you are compatible with each other. The tax person may refer you to someone with more experience in your field, a small business specialist, or to someone who is less expensive yet still knowledgeable and so more cost effective for you.

You are interviewing the tax specialist, too, so if you aren't comfortable with the person, simply say "Thanks, but no thanks" and try someone else. It is important that you not feel intimidated, and that you can ask all those questions you feel are "dumb." We don't learn if we don't ask! Talking about how we spend our money and run our business is a very personal thing and it is important that we have a good relationship with this person so we can ask ANY financial question.

DO ask if the specialist has experience appearing before the IRS — audits do happen occasionally (one chance in 70 on average). Make sure the tax specialist would represent you in an audit. Also find out if they will accept responsibility for any errors on your return, and pay any penalties and interest that may be incurred.

Check Your Insurance

After I had been sewing for pay for awhile, I casually asked our family insurance agent about coverage for my business. I was shocked to learn that our homeowner's insurance policy did not cover any business-related claims. Indeed, it is possible that running a business from your home voids the coverage of your policy altogether. I quickly added a rider to our homeowner's policy that covered liability and business personal property.

I am not crazy about spending a lot of money on insurance, but I feel these are necessities:

♦ **Liability** - for bodily injury. If a client slips on my stairs and is injured, liability covers the injuries, and me, should my client sue.

♦ **Business personal property** - Covers business equipment (desk, chair, sewing machines, etc.) should it be lost or damaged by fire or theft. This also covers my clients' property when it is in my care. Imagine how tragic it would be if a client's $1000 designer gown awaiting alterations were stolen or damaged by fire!

My insurance agent reported that the above are often part of a business insurance package that includes many features desirable to a small business owner — often a less expensive way to get good coverage.

♦ **Disability insurance** - Income paid should I be injured or ill and unable to work. Since my family depends on my income and would suffer if I were unable to work for an extended period, I have disability insurance. I was lucky to find that I could purchase this through my husband's policy at work. As this is generally a costly form of insurance, hinging on my husband's policy was a real savings for me. I feel this insurance is not of value when your income is small. However, as your income becomes more important to your family, your need for disability insurance increases. My insurance agent noted that this insurance is priced according to the risk involved in the occupation. Dressmaking is certainly less hazardous than washing high-rise windows, and the premium reflects this risk. I feel you have three choices with disability - have enough money saved to see you through an extended illness; live uninsured on the ragged edge; or buy disability insurance.

My insurance agent said, "Most importantly, contact your in-surance agent first to find what is and is not covered on your existing homeowner's or renter's policy. All insurance companies and all policies are different. Since your home is probably your most valuable asset, and even more valuable now that it is also your work space, make sure your homeowner's coverage is current with inflation."

Start-up Checklist

Use the following list to check off when you have accomplished the important preliminary steps to starting a successful business:

☐ Check into local permits, licenses, trade name regulations, sales tax, zoning.

☐ Make a business plan.

☐ Set up your business office.

☐ Order business cards, stationery, garment labels.

☐ Talk to a tax specialist.

☐ Investigate insurance.

Now you are ready to start the fun things like organizing your sewing space!

CHAPTER 7

Organize Your Sewing Space

My First Sewing Space

I now have the perfect work space for my business, but I started in a small area of my home as you may have to do. I began my business in a corner of the family room in our first home. I had children running in and out and confusion everywhere.

My equipment consisted of my sewing machine, ironing board, and a cardboard cutting board that I used on top of the family room eating bar. I created an L-shaped work space by placing an extra table (purchased with Green Stamps) next to my free-arm sewing machine table. An old brass floor lamp became extra lighting and I borrowed the wastebasket from our bedroom.

I purchased (from a discount store) plastic chests with many drawers for storage of small sewing aids, and stacked these under the L-shaped work space. I placed a bulletin board in front of my machine to hold guide sheets and messages. My chair was metal with a pillow on top. I did all fittings in our bedroom using a mirror on the back of a door. You can see that these were modest beginnings!

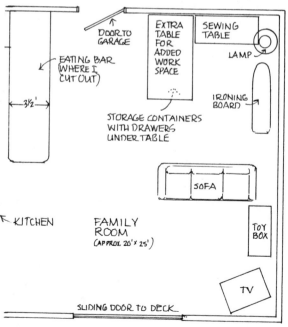

DOOR TO GARAGE

EXTRA TABLE FOR ADDED WORK SPACE

SEWING TABLE

LAMP

EATING BAR (WHERE I CUT OUT)

—3½'—

IRONING BOARD

STORAGE CONTAINERS WITH DRAWERS UNDER TABLE

SOFA

KITCHEN

FAMILY ROOM (APPROX. 20' x 25')

TOY BOX

TV

SLIDING DOOR TO DECK

In 1977 we built a new home, including a wonderful little apartment for my mom. I had a 16′ × 20′ sewing room with a door to close off the mess. It was off the family room so I could be close to my family even while working. Now I could really get organized.

In 1984 Mom left us to go live with her sister and I took over her apartment for a sewing studio. My children were older so I had time to take on more clients. Interestingly, each time I moved to a larger space, my business expanded too.

I still work in that studio, and have built my business to what it is today. When Pati Palmer asked me to create a book and a video on dressmaking, I was thrilled! My ship had come in! I used my video money to remodel the studio into a beautiful, all-white area — something I had only dreamed about — and then used it when filming the video.

Welcome to My New Studio

I have two rooms with 800 square feet. Our home is on a lovely wooded lot, and we have many floor-to-ceiling windows so my work area has natural light and nice views. I also have a private entrance for the studio. I no longer have clients coming through the family part of the house. I have taught my family to say, "I will go down to the studio and let you in." This is important to me for business success in my home.

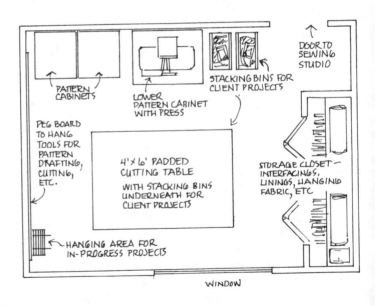

CUT ROOM

PATTERN CABINETS

LOWER PATTERN CABINET WITH PRESS

STACKING BINS FOR CLIENT PROJECTS

DOOR TO SEWING STUDIO

PEG BOARD TO HANG TOOLS FOR PATTERN DRAFTING, CUTTING, ETC.

4′ × 6′ PADDED CUTTING TABLE

WITH STACKING BINS UNDERNEATH FOR CLIENT PROJECTS

STORAGE CLOSET — INTERFACINGS, LININGS, HANGING FABRIC, ETC

HANGING AREA FOR IN-PROGRESS PROJECTS

WINDOW

SEWING STUDIO

YOU CAN SEE ALL THIS IN MY
VIDEO - SEWING TO SUCCESS!

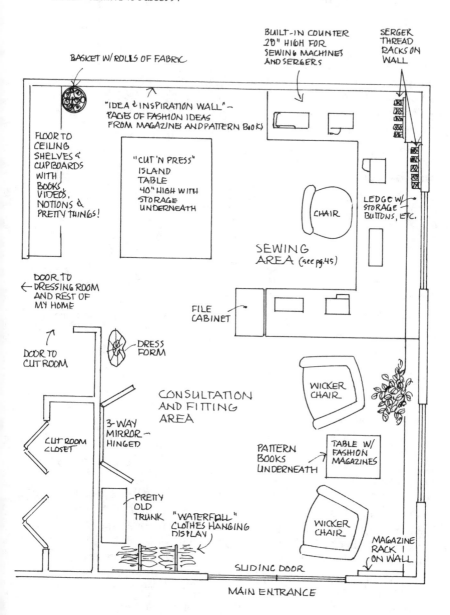

BASKET W/ ROLLS OF FABRIC

BUILT-IN COUNTER
28" HIGH FOR
SEWING MACHINES
AND SERGERS

SERGER
THREAD
RACKS ON
WALL

"IDEA & INSPIRATION WALL" -
PAGES OF FASHION IDEAS
FROM MAGAZINES AND PATTERN BOOKS

FLOOR TO
CEILING
SHELVES &
CUPBOARDS
WITH
BOOKS,
VIDEOS,
NOTIONS &
PRETTY THINGS!

"CUT 'N PRESS"
ISLAND
TABLE
40" HIGH WITH
STORAGE
UNDERNEATH

CHAIR

SEWING
AREA (see pg. 45)

LEDGE W/
STORAGE
BUTTONS, ETC.

DOOR TO
← DRESSING ROOM
AND REST OF
MY HOME

FILE
CABINET

DOOR TO
CUT ROOM

DRESS
FORM

CONSULTATION
AND FITTING
AREA

WICKER
CHAIR

CUT ROOM
CLOSET

3-WAY
MIRROR -
HINGED

PATTERN
BOOKS
UNDERNEATH

TABLE W/
FASHION
MAGAZINES

PRETTY
OLD
TRUNK

"WATERFALL"
CLOTHES HANGING
DISPLAY

WICKER
CHAIR

MAGAZINE
RACK
ON WALL

SLIDING DOOR

MAIN ENTRANCE

43

My clients enter a comfortable sitting area with two chairs and a table holding magazines and pattern books where we do all business planning. I have bulletin boards filled with fashion clippings for inspiration. It is a cheery area! Opposite the chairs is a fitting area with a mirror. The client is never out of this area except to walk around the corner to the bathroom to change for fittings.

Next to the mirror I have a grid wall system where I hang in-progress clothing. I found this sturdy unit at a commercial display store. It must be bolted to the wall, but it holds many garments without taking up valuable floor space.

"WATERFALL" WALL SYSTEM

Lynette Black, author of the Palmer/Pletsch Trends Bulletin, **The Newest in Sewing Room Design** (see page 123), helped me design my sewing area.

At each end I have modular cabinets similar to those used in kitchens, with a custom table that is actually high-pressure laminate countertop that attaches to the walls. This gives great stability for vibration-free sewing and serging. I had my table built to house all of my machines, and for me the U-shape is ideal. The braces under the counter top are tapered so I can swivel quickly from one machine to another without bumping my knees. Holes were drilled in the counter top back and finished with grommets to drop the cords through - no more cord clutter! What a great idea!

The Sewing Area

In the sewing "U", directly in front of the window, I have placed the machine I use most. I can enjoy my view and get natural light. By using many machines, I improve my productivity:

1. I use my computer machine for general sewing.
2. On my right is an old machine with a buttonhole attachment that makes wonderful buttonholes. That is all I ask it to do. I save precious time by having the buttonholer always ready.
3. On my far right is a serger. I use it primarily for finishing seams, and I like to move to the right when I am working.
4. To the left of machine #1 is another serger set up for rolled hems. When I have more than one garment going and do not want to change thread on machine #3, I set it for seaming or edge finishing.
5. Machine #5 is a spare serger in case anything else breaks down.
6. Number 6 is my trusty old machine that I purchased when I first started my business. It has worked faithfully for 17 years and I am sentimentally attached to it. I use my sweet little machine to make piping. It has a wonderful zipper foot with a quilting bar attached, and I can instantly make perfect piping and quickly apply it to a garment. I pipe many garments and make yards of piping in a year, so it is a valuable timesaver for me.

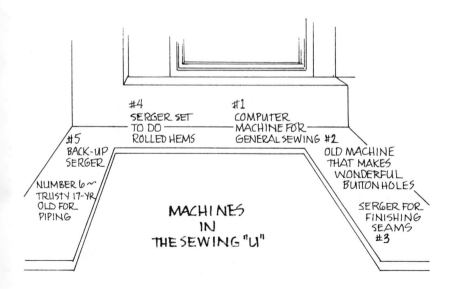

My Perfect Chair

In the center of the sewing area is my perfect chair. The seat and back are adjustable, it swivels, it rocks, it leans forward, it leans backward. It has wheels that travel on carpeting so I can roll between machines. Most importantly, it is comfortable for sitting for long periods while sewing and it provides good back support. My chair was expensive but it is worth it - no more backaches!

I went to every office supply store and discount office furniture store and sat in chairs until I found one I liked and could afford. You can pay up to $500; I paid $110 at a discount office equipment store. Sears and J.C. Penney catalogs are also good sources if your choices for the "sit test" are limited. I think I sat in at least 100 chairs before I bought this one. My family thought I had gone crazy. "Mom, it's only a chair!" A good resource would be your chiropractor or orthopedic doctor. They understand what the human body needs for comfort when sitting a lot.

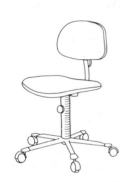

The Pressing Island

My pressing island is still in transition. I took two old chests of drawers, painted them white, and placed them back to back. (They have to be the same height or you must add spacers.) I padded my "cut 'n press" board (see page 107), covered it and placed it on top. I use the drawer space to store pressing equipment and sewing notions. The chest height creates a work surface that is much more comfortable to cut at than a lower table.

My Special Cut Room

Last but not least is my cutting room. This room is so critical that I could not tear it apart when I remodeled the rest of the studio. It is still in its old clothes, but soon to be redressed. The room is 12' × 14' and its primary occupant is my 4' × 6' cutting table. Under the cutting table are stacking plastic bins that hold each client's individual projects. A large window provides natural light. The end wall is covered with pegboard that holds every tool that can hang. Clothing repairs and alterations also hang on this pegboard. Along the next wall are three fabric store pattern cabinets, with see-through plastic storage boxes stacked on top. I like to see inside my storage and I just stack until it reaches the ceiling. On a lower pattern cabinet I have my ironing press (see page 106) that I use for fusing. Because it's next to the cutting board I can just reach over and flip it on and fuse right after cutting.

At the end of the cutting room is a closet where I hang all fabric that has been preshrunk at the dry cleaner and I stack bolts of interfacing and fabric on the shelves.

A Practical Carpet

I have a commercial, tightly-woven, plush carpet on my floor, and it has a thick pad under it. Because the floor is concrete and because I stand so much, my designer advised that I carpet for comfort. This carpeting does not eat pins as you might imagine. I spilled pins on the carpet samples to test before I made my decision.

Dirty carpeting makes dirty clothing, which is bad for business, so I ask all clients to remove their shoes when they enter. When we try on the garments I make sure their shoes are clean before they walk onto the carpet.

Remember, this is the "perfect" room for me, not the room I started in. It has taken me 17 years to get to this point because I had to earn all money that was spent on remodeling and on equipment. Be patient, work hard, and dream. Dreams do come true!

Creative Work Spaces for You

- ◆ Corner of family room, kitchen, office or den
- ◆ Corner of master bedroom if still usable for night sewing
- ◆ Laundry room or basement
- ◆ Closet where you can close the door on your mess
- ◆ Corner of a garage that has been enclosed and heated
- ◆ A room or a small building added on to your property
- ◆ Barn or other existing outer building
- ◆ Van or motor home - ideal for alterations specialists who can travel to their clients!

CHAPTER 8

How to Make Money: Pricing For Profit

As I talk with other sewing professionals, we agree that pricing is an awkward issue. They all began as I did, "guesstimating" what we thought a project was worth. I can now give you specific information to use as a guide for pricing your work. I also realize that pricing is an individual and evolutionary process, and you must go through some of the steps yourself. But I can help you do it faster!

My Experience With Pricing

I began being organized about pricing in 1978 when I first met Pati Palmer and Susan Pletsch. They were creating a huge traveling fashion show and were hiring dressmakers to produce the clothes. At that time I was billing about minimum wage of $2.50 per hour. When Palmer and Pletsch said they were paying $5 per hour I jumped with joy! Then I went to work!

I kept a clock and notepad by my machine and logged the time I spent on each project. I included telephone time (talking to Pati or Susan about the project), thinking, planning, cutting, sewing and delivery time. I learned how long it took me to make specific items. I found a blazer made with fusible interfacings took me eight hours. This did not include unusual pockets, vents, bound buttonholes, and the fabric had to be "no-fail" like tweed.

I began to use the "base-price-plus-details" method of pricing and developed a price sheet with my eight-hour blazer costing $40 (8 hours × $5.00 per hour). As my experience and speed increased, so did my price and my profit. I still use the "base-price-plus-details" method. It helps my clients make decisions about the final price by knowing the costs of the details they add.

I am including my price sheets (see pages 56, 57, 64). Don't be shocked by how much I charge. I find most home-sewers underestimate the value of their time, especially women with little or no work experience. It is very important to set realistic prices so you can cover your costs and make a profit. That's what we're talking about — doing what we love for a profit!

Factors Affecting Price

My prices are high but, for my market, they are realistic. There are many custom dressmakers in cities more expensive than mine who make twice what I do. Prices are very "geographically sensitive." I could charge more if I were located in downtown Portland, Oregon. I am in a suburb, so my clientele is more financially conservative.

Prices are affected by:

1. Urban or rural location, city size, local economy
2. Local competition
3. Sewing skills, experience and speed.

Study Pricing - Make Comparisons

To give you an idea of costs in your area, department stores and dry cleaners often publish rates for repairs and alterations. A custom dressmaker can often price competitively with those businesses because of the low overhead in a home-based business. Not all custom dressmakers are in competition with you. Your service and skills may deserve a higher rate. Be competitive and do not undercharge for your quality work.

I am a member of the Custom Clothing Guild of Oregon (see page 120); and, of course, pricing is a common topic in our group. Often our new members are billing at a low rate of $4 to $5 per hour. As we counsel them and as their skills increase, so do their prices. Currently our group's average price is about $10 per hour, but some of our members are now charging $15 to $20 per hour.

Many dressmakers begin by comparing their prices to ready-to-wear clothing prices. This comparison can give an erroneous concept of your service and worth. You offer individual fit; ready-to-wear offers standardized fit. You offer choices in design; ready-to-wear decides the design for the customer. You can use fabric the customer loves; ready-to-wear has chosen the fabric. Why, then, do dressmakers compare themselves to ready-made clothing? Because this is the clothing arena in which the public has been trained to shop.

As dressmakers offering personal service, we must be educated in fashion, line, quality, design and technique, so we can be a more attractive service than ready-made clothing. Our goal should be to provide an alternative to mass-produced clothing. Our goal should **not** be to match their prices.

"Sewing as a Business" Workshop

I was part of an innovative project called **Sewing as a Business Workshop**, jointly-funded by Mississippi Extension Home Economics, the American Home Sewing Association, and Extension Service - USDA. This was an educational program designed to train and assist home-based entrepreneurs in establishing profitable home-based sewing businesses. The workshop focused on the business skills, marketing skills and new technology needed to develop a **profitable** home-based sewing business.

Beth Duncan, Extension Clothing and Textile Specialist in Mississippi, feels that sewing professionals often focus on the creative aspects of a home-based sewing business and ignore the business side. She sees the key factor for success to be learning and understanding the business side well enough to make the creative side pay. Beth says:

1. It is **essential** to be prepared businesswise.
2. You must find professionals who can guide you in the business aspects of your new business.
3. Seek new information and continue to learn about business matters.

The 145 graduates of this program in Mississippi responded that the workshops:

♦ Helped them feel professional
♦ Gave them self-esteem
♦ Helped them to view themselves as successful business people
♦ Gave them confidence.

Their enthusiasm and new business knowledge have helped them to raise their incomes by an average of 52% following the workshops. One star graduate who had been earning under $500 per year has developed a new serger product that is now nationally distributed, netting her over $100,000 this year and employing many others. What a success story she is! (See page 120 for more information on "Sewing as a Business" Workshops.)

Pricing For Profit

In the **Sewing as a Business** workbook, Beth Duncan did such a good job discussing pricing that I am going to quote her directly. Thanks Beth, for making a complex issue simple.

Sewing for Profit

In a home-based sewing business, the total cost of producing a product or service is composed of three major factors:

♦ Direct costs
♦ Salary
♦ Overhead/operating expenses.

This is the information that should be used for setting your prices. The more exact you figure your costs and set prices, the greater your chances for a continued and profitable business.

Direct costs

Include all the materials and supplies that go into making a product. In a home-based sewing business, in most cases, the customer is responsible for supplying fabrics, patterns, and notions. However, there may be times when you use your own zipper, thread, interfacing, buttons, etc. These costs may seem incidental, but they can add up quickly. Before you know it, you could be using a couple dollars worth of your own supplies in every garment you make.

Salary

You should pay yourself a set salary. After all, that's why you're in business, **to make money**. The following are two ways sewing professionals determine salary:

1. **By the job (task)** - Develop a complete list of the various sewing tasks. Determine how long it takes you to complete each task. Each sewing project can then be broken down into tasks that are added up to give a total time figure in hours. Decide how much you want to pay yourself an hour. For each sewing project, multiply the total time figure by $ per hour to determine your salary. (See page 55 for the Construction Price List.)

2. **By the hour** - Keep an accurate account of the total amount of time required to complete a sewing project. This means keeping a written log of what you did and the amount of time required. Decide how much you want to pay yourself an hour and multiply the total time figure by $ per hour to determine your salary. (See page 54 for the Base Garment Construction Price List.)

Overhead/operating expenses

Include all the costs of running a business that are not directly related to the actual production of a specific product or service. In a home-based sewing business, this would include taxes, advertising, rent, insurance, business permits, maintenance and repair of equipment, business supplies, sewing supplies/notions/equipment, utilities (electricity, telephone, etc.), professional assistance (accountant, attorney, etc.) and other costs related to the overall operation of the business.

Two methods used to determine overhead/operating expenses:

1. **Average method** - If you have been in business for at least a year, it should be fairly easy for you to pull all of your overhead figures together to arrive at an average hourly cost. But if you are just starting, you will have to do some guesstimating. To illustrate how overhead figures fit into the pricing picture, let's assume that your annual business overhead costs are $3,000, and you're working 1,000 hours per year on your business. That means your average hourly overhead rate is $3 ($3,000 ÷ 1,000). For example, a skirt that took two hours to complete would have a $6.00 overhead cost added to the total charge.

2. **Percent Method** - Determine your total overhead expenses for a year. Divide the total amount of your direct costs plus salary for a year into the first figure. For example, if you have received $5,400 last year for direct costs and salary and you had $1,500 in overhead costs, you would divide 1500 by 5400 to get an overhead of 28%. That translates to 28 cents which should be added to every dollar you charge.

Start now to document all the overhead costs that will affect the profitability of your business in the months and years to come. At the beginning of each new business year analyze your overhead costs, then adjust your prices accordingly.

Pricing the Product

Up to this point we have discussed how to determine your Direct Costs = A, Salary = B, and Overhead Expenses = C. To determine the price you charge your customer for a sewing project, you add these three figures together. In other words:

A + B + C = PRICE

An alternative formula for pricing, called the "hourly rate formula," takes a different approach. The hourly rate is determined through a calculation based on desired income, time and expenses. Decide how much you would like to net for the year, then estimate the number of working hours per week and multiply this figure by the number of work weeks. Next add your direct costs and overhead expenses for the year and divide by the number of working hours per year. Add this hourly figure to the first hourly figure to get the final hourly rate you will need to charge to realize your desired net income at year's end.

EXAMPLE: Let's say you desire $6,000 net income, and you work part-time 20 hours per week × 50 weeks, or 1,000 work hours per year. Divide net income by 1,000 work hours to get a $6 hourly rate for your time. Now add up direct costs and overhead expenses for the year. Let's assume they are $3,800. Divide this expense figure by 1,000 hours to get an hourly expense rate of $3.80. Add this to the $6.00 figure to get a total of $9.80, or the amount you must charge per hour to realize $6,000 net income at year's end.

Using this formula you have already taken into account direct costs and overhead expenses, thus to determine the price of a sewing project you simply multiply the hourly rate by the total number of hours spent on the project. In other words:

(Hourly Rate) × (# of Hours) = PRICE

Practice calculating prices using different approaches. Analyze the prices, keeping in mind that location, reputation, skill level and competition are also factors to consider when determining a pricing system for your business. Once you decide on a pricing system, use the same approach for all customers. This will avoid confusion in setting rates and avoid problems with pricing differences that could occur.

BASE GARMENT CONSTRUCTION PRICE LIST

Garment	Time (Hours)	$5/Hour	$6/Hour	$8/Hour
Skirt: A-Line or Straight				
Unlined	4	20	24	32
Lined	5	25	30	40
Skirt: Pleated	4½+	22.50+	27+	36+
Skirt: Plaid Fabric	4¼+	21.25+	25.50+	34+
Blouse: Long Sleeves, Cuffs, Collar	4½+	22.50+	27+	36+
Blouse: Lace, Ruffles, Pleats	5+	25+	30+	40+
Dress: Chemise, Short Sleeves	6	30	36	48
Dress: Waistline, Long Sleeves	7½	37.50	45	60
Dress: Full Skirt, Floor-length	8½	42.50	51	68
Jacket: Unlined	8	40	48	64
Jacket: Tailored, Lined	10	50	60	80
Coat: Tailored	12	60	72	96
Pants: Lined	5½	27.50	33	44
Pants: Unlined	4½	22.50	27	36
Bridal Gown	20	100	120	160
Bridal Slip	2	10	12	16
Bridesmaids	15	75	90	120
Mother-of-the-bride	10	50	60	80
Evening	15	75	90	120

Courtesy of Mississippi Cooperative Extension Service
(Adapted from information provided by the Maryland Extension Service.)

The **Base Garment Construction Price List** prices 20 different types of garments. You can use this list to estimate the price of a garment for a client.

Use the two lists together to figure an accurate final garment fee that includes the extras. Add extras from the "Construction Price List" to the base garment price.

NOTE: These charts reflect current pricing in Mississippi where the charts were assembled. Your local rate may be higher or lower. You can use the chart to figure rates that are not shown. If you are charging $12 per hour, simply double the numbers in the $6 column.

CONSTRUCTION PRICE LIST

Construction Technique	Time (Hours)	$5/Hour	$6/Hour	$8/Hour
Initial measurements and evaluation	½	2.50	3	4
Help with pattern and fabric selection	½+	2.50+	3+	4+
Pattern Alterations	1 to 2	5 to 10	6 to 12	8 to 16
Pretreating Fabric	¼ to ½	1.25 to 2.50	1.50 to 3	2 to 4
Layout, Cutting, Marking	½ to 1	2.50 to 5	3 to 6	4 to 8
Matching Plaids	½	2.50	3	4
Seams and Darts	½+	2.50 to 5	3 to 6	4 to 8
Collars	½ to 1	2.50 to 5	3 to 6	4 to 8
Neck Facing	¾	3.75	4.50	6
Sleeve (Set-in)	1	5	6	8
Two-piece	1¼	5.25	7.50	10
Gathered	1¼	6.25	7.50	10
Cuffs	½+	2.50+	3+	4+
Armhole Facings	1	5	6	8
Zipper — Fly-front	1	5	6	8
Hand-picked	¾	3.75	4.50	6
Lapped or Centered	½	2.50	3	4
Front Opening Band	½ to 1	2.50 to 5	3 to 6	4 to 8
Pockets — Welt	1 to 2	5 to 10	6 to 12	8 to 16
Patch	½ to 1	2.50 to 5	3 to 6	4 to 8
Waistband	½	2.50	3	4
Elastic Casings	¼ to ½	1.25 to 2.50	1.50 to 3	2 to 4
Buttonholes — Bound	—	1.25/Each	1.50/Each	2/Each
Machine	6 minutes	.50/Each	.60/Each	.80/Each
Sew on Buttons —				
By Machine	—	.25/Each	.30/Each	.40/Each
By Hand	—	.40/Each	.45/Each	.60/Each
Snaps, Hooks and Eyes	—	.75/Set	.90/Set	1.20/Set
Belt — Buckle	¾	3.75	4.50	6
Tie	½	2.50	3	4
Topstitching	½+	2.50+	3+	4+
Pleats and Tucks	½+	2.50+	3+	4+
Underlining	1 to 2½	5 to 12.50	6 to 15	8 to 20
Lining — Skirt or Pants	1 to 2	5 to 10	6 to 12	8 to 16
Coat or Jacket	2 to 4	10 to 20	12 to 24	16 to 32
Simple Dress	1½ to 3	7.50 to 15	9 to 18	12 to 24
Cover Buttons	—	.25/Each	.30/Each	.40/Each
Custom Shoulder Pads	1	5	6	8
Hem — Edge Finish	1¼	6.25	7.50	10
No Edge Finish	¾	3.75	4.50	6
Follow-up Fitting	½+	2.50+	3+	4+

Courtesy of Mississippi Cooperative Extension Service.
(Adapted from information from Iowa State University Extension Service.)

My Price List

Now compare my price list:

for **KATHLEEN SPIKE**

PRICE SHEET

SKIRTS
Unlined basic straight $50.00
Lined with inside pocket $57.00
Extra pleats, vents, belt loops,
   pockets, darts $5.00
Welt pockets (each) $9.50
Lined and underlined straight skirt . . $75.00
Four-gore skirt w/o zipper $47.50
Four-gore w/zipper $55.00
Four-gore w/zipper and lined $65.00

DRESSES
Basic price $75.00
Added design features (pleats,
   tucks, plackets, quilting,
   buttonholes) . . . . $7.50-$15.00
Design proofs of original drafting . . $30.00
Per hour for copying
   and designing $15.00

BLOUSES
Summer style pull over $35.00
Short sleeves with opening $45.00
Long sleeves, no cuffs, no collar . . . $75.00
Long sleeves, collar buttons,
   simple placket $95.00
Added design features
   (per feature) . . . . $7.50-$15.00

SHAWL-COLLARED JACKETS
Unlined $75.00
Lined $85.00

TAILORED JACKETS
Unlined $90.00
Lined (base price) $120.00
Each added pocket, vent, or flap . . $9.50

CARDIGAN JACKETS
Unlined (base price) $50.00
Lined (base price) $90.00
Each added pocket, vent, or flap . . $9.50

COATS
Collarless (base price) $85.00
Shawl style (base price) $95.00
Tailored style (base price) $125.00
Each added pocket, vent, or flap . . $9.50

ULTRASUEDE®
Unlined straight skirt $82.50
Lined skirt $90.00
Tailored jacket (base price) $125.00
Lined, tailored coat (base price) . $150.00
Lined shawl coat (base price) . . . $135.00
Lined collarless coat (base price) $100.00
Back pocket or vent $9.50
Bound buttonholes $7.50
Jumper . . . . $50.00-$75.00
Piping $10.00

MISCELLANEOUS
Plaid garment cutouts - jacket $10.00
  - skirts $7.50
Stripes $7.50
Fee for working on white wool
   gabardine or flannel $7.50
Seams added $7.50
Applied piping, custom made $7.50
Bound buttonholes - woven $9.00
  - Ultrasuede® $7.50
Sleeves $15.00
Mock-ups . . . . $25.00-$50.00

Design · Dressmaking · Instruction
1880 S.W. Heiney Road
Gresham, OR 97080
(503) 665-6505

MISCELLANEOUS (continued)

Hand sewn collar $7.50
Copying master patterns $10.00
Size 16 and over (per garment) . . . $15.00
Shoulder pads - uncovered $5.00
  - covered $6.00
  - covered and installed
    in any garment $7.50
  - covered and installed
    in retail garment $10.00
House calls/hourly shopping $15.00
Consultation fees (new client
  consultation fee is waived
  if project is accepted) $25.00
Design linings - jackets $10.00
  - skirts $5.00
Jumpsuit (easy collar, no cuffs,
  elastic waist) $80.00
Wardrobe planning (per hour) $15.00

ALTERATIONS

Hems 60" or less $10.00
Replace skirt zipper $9.00
  jean zipper $10.00
Taper skirt or leg side seams 15.00

NOTE: Prices are approximate, depending on fabric type and complexity, and subject to change without notice. All findings and supplies are an additional charge. I cannot be responsible for fabrics left at the studio over six months.

Effective
July 1, 1989

NOTE: For Pants Price List see page 64.

Notice at the bottom of my price sheet that "Prices are subject to change without notice." You should update your price sheet yearly and date it. Simply hand your client a new price sheet the next time you see her. Any garment that is started before a new price increase is charged out at the old price. Note, too, that all findings and supplies are an additional charge, and that you cannot be responsible for fabrics left in the studio over six months.

Discussing Price With the Client

I never discuss my hourly charge with a client. I talk in piece prices and increment prices, giving an approximate figure or price range for a total. "The finished price, labor only, will be $120 to $140." I want them to understand that this business is like painting. An artist does not sit down before a canvas and know exactly what the finished portrait will look like. I feel I am commissioned to do a work of art with each garment and I need some artistic flexibility in the final price. I refuse to be boxed in for the sake of money.

I work to develop a repeat clientele because the more I work for a person, the fewer unknowns there are. I create more designs or patterns that can be used again and again, and I am more clear about her style, body shape and needs. A new client has to be educated in my style of service. I spend a lot of time teaching each client, making her aware of her own style, colors and the fabrications appropriate for her. I like to cultivate clients and keep them. This is worth dollars in profit to me.

Getting Paid

When I work with a new client, I require a 20% deposit on the first project. That way I am sure they are committed to the concept of this garment, and that they understand that this is a serious business arrangement. I don't ask this of my existing clients; we understand one another. I never deposit any initial money I receive until the garment is completed. I like to create my own deadlines, and if I know the money is waiting for me I work harder and faster.

Do not deliver a garment without receiving full payment. Not for any excuse, nor any circumstance. You are a "cash only" business, with no credit extended. If you choose to accept charge cards, remember the bank will charge you a percentage for processing.

CHAPTER 9

Specializing Can Mean Greater Profit

Begin With General Dressmaking

I think the average dressmaker starts in business with no thoughts of specializing. She wants and needs to accept as many projects as she can to gain experience and to build a profit base. A general dressmaking business is actually a step toward specializing. In order to specialize, you need to become very proficient in one area of dressmaking.

Think of general dressmaking as starting in an entry level position in a large company and working your way to the top. You will learn most of what you need to know for success along the way. Specialization in the beginning can limit your horizons by limiting your exposure to technical and professional growth.

My First Specialty Was Tailoring

I specialized in tailoring after five years of general dressmaking. When fashion shifted from tailored jackets and blazers to dresses and skirts, I had to open my mind to doing more dressmaking than tailoring. I found my clients had all the jackets they wanted. They needed me now to sew dresses and skirts to wear with their tailored blazers. It was important that I was aware enough of fashion trends to recognize this change. I had to adjust my thinking and redirect my talents to flow with the fashion tide.

Specializing can create a "feast or famine" situation. Thankfully I always live with the "Plan B Possibility." If Plan A is no longer viable, I always have Plan B on the back burner! I went on to develop a coat clientele because my love of tailoring wanted to survive! I now do more tailored separates and coats than I do jackets or blazers. I flexed with the fashion trends, and so my specialty survived with a few changes.

I discovered my specialty when I sewed for the Palmer/Pletsch fashion show in 1978. I found that I loved tailoring and natural-fiber fabrics, and

59

Palmer and Pletsch introduced me to the **best** of both. I decided (and wrote down) that my goal was to become the best tailoring dressmaker and tailoring teacher that I could be. I focused on those two goals with incredible energy.

I put myself in every available situation that would promote my tailoring and teaching of tailoring. I practiced what I preached too. I became the best-dressed tailor/dressmaker and teacher that I could afford to be. I read every fashion magazine from cover to cover, focusing on just one part of a tailored garment, circling every lapel for example, and noting the differences. I studied men's and women's tailored clothing by looking at magazines, catalogs and garments in stores. I read every technical book and took every class offered so I could improve my knowledge and skills.

Specialties can cause seasonal changes in business. If you choose to sew bridal wear, you may be swamped in spring and summer and slow in winter. In the slow times you could fill in with another idea, say holiday specialties, or do alterations, or take an extended vacation!

When you specialize, your speed and skill in producing your chosen product should increase tremendously. If they don't and you continue to struggle, try another specialty. When speed and skill increase, you can produce more **and** charge more for your services, so profits increase too.

My Second Specialty - Pants

My next specialty was fitting and sewing pants. I saw a need within my customer base and decided to fill it. I did the same type of research and studying for pants that I had done for tailoring. This time though, I knew I had selected a market niche that would continue to grow. Pants may come and go as a fashion statement, but they are always a part of my clients' wardrobes.

When I began focusing on pants in 1981, I grew to love it so much that I co-authored a book, **Fast Fashion Jeans for Family Fun** (see page 122). I became an expert on and still sew custom-fitted jeans. Two pairs were picked up last week! Jeans may be less important fashionwise, but pants continue to increase in popularity.

Now I travel and teach pant fitting and sewing for Palmer/Pletsch, and I highly recommend their book, **Pants For Any Body**, and the slacks fitting pattern they have designed for McCall Pattern company.

I advertise and promote my specialties. It's easier to get a customer's attention promoting a specific concept like pants than a general idea like dressmaking. I created the following flyer and letter to send to everyone on my client list. I also give them to new clients so they are aware of my skills.

Within my pants specialty you can see from my price list (page 64) that I do a variety of things. I don't like to be bored! Home-sewers even come to me for a custom basic pants pattern that they can take home and sew. They also come for pants fitting and sewing instruction. I generally create a custom basic pants pattern for a client and then design all of her fashion pants from that basic. I made 30 pairs of pants for one client in one year!

Training for my specialties took time and energy, but I have increased my proficiency, my credibility, my speed and my profits. I love the business I have developed for myself! I can see all of my past hard work really paying off.

Possible Specialties to Ponder:

- Alterations
- Antique clothing
- Bridal
- Banners, kites, sails
- Career wardrobes
- Clothing for the handicapped
- Costumes
- Crafts, consignment or custom
- Custom embellished sweatshirts
- Custom sweats
- Decorator accessories
- Decorator pillows
- Doll clothing
- Dolls
- Draperies
- Embellished clothing
- Embroidery
- Evening wear
- Fashion accessories
- French hand sewing
- Golf or tennis wear
- Half-size clothing

- Holiday specialties
- Lingerie
- Menswear
- Monogramming
- Pants fitting and sewing
- Quilted clothing
- Quilts
- Skiwear
- Slipcovers
- Smocking
- Square dance clothing
- Stuffed animals or toys
- Swim, dance or aerobic wear
- Tailoring
- Travel wardrobes
- Ultrasuede® garments
- Uniforms
- Upholstery
- Western wear
- Window coverings
- Window shades

for
**KATHLEEN
SPIKE**

CUSTOM PANTS SERVICE

Thank you for inquiring about my custom pant designs. This letter will help you understand my philosophy and style of service.

I believe that few of us can afford to be impulsive shoppers. The stakes are too high and mistakes too costly. Pants are a fashionable and necessary part of most women's wardrobes.

From a professional viewpoint, I feel the choices we have in the retail marketplace are very limited. The prices are high, the quality is low, and the fit is seldom flattering or comfortable. Pants are usually a desperation purchase. We choose to overlook the imperfections because we think we have no other options.

I offer you an alternative. My service offers the right decision for you, quality pants construction, individualized fit, and personal wardrobe planning. I can offer you a garment that should fashionably last five to ten years, providing your figure does not change dramatically.

At our first appointment, which will take 20 to 30 minutes, I will take your measurements over the undergarments that you usually wear under pants. Appropriate shoes are also required. We will discuss your figure type, lifestyle, and past experience with the fit of your pants. We will decide which design will be suitable for you. I will explain where to shop for appropriate fabric and what types of fabrics to buy. I suggest you go shopping and, at our next appointment, bring fabric samples to be evaluated. You will need fabric fiber content, price, width, and store name for each sample.

Next, I will design your pattern, cut it in muslin, and sew the muslin together. Our second appointment will include fitting and alteration adjustments. This can take as much as an hour or as little as 15 minutes. If you have already purchased an appropriate piece of fabric, bring it at this time. If you still must shop for fabric, you can mail it to me or drop it by my studio.

The fitting of the fashion pant during our third appointment can take fifteen minutes to one hour. Come prepared to stay an hour and have something to read. When all fine-tuning is completed, we will make another appointment for you to pick up your finished pants.

You will have thirty days to test the design and to become accustomed to my interpretation of a good fit in your new fashion pants. Keep in mind that most people will feel strange wearing a properly fitted pair of pants — no baggy derriere, no crotch crunch or bag, no tummy tugging. A properly fitted pant skims over the curves without stress points, and it does not hug the body. A looser fit is more sophisticated, flattering and comfortable. The right fashion fabric also contributes a great deal to fit.

Once this highly personalized measuring and fitting phase is completed, pants can be made almost at a moment's notice. I then require only one quick fitting and one delivery appointment.

My goal as a custom clothier is to have a happy clientele. I know this is possible if I develop a comfortable communication with each of you. Your critique of the design, fit and construction can only help me to serve you better. Remember, my custom-fitted, custom sewn pants are guaranteed to please.

Design · Dressmaking · Instruction
1880 S.W. Heiney Road
Gresham, OR 97080
(503) 665-6505

Kathleen Spike

for
**KATHLEEN
SPIKE**

PANTS PRICE LIST

CUSTOM PANTS PATTERNS

Home-sewers $75.00
    Includes pattern and valuable instruction
    sheets on sewing techniques: zippers,
    waistbands, sewing order
    Additional muslin fabric charge . . . $8.00
Home-sewers (hip size over 46") . . $90.00
    Additional muslin fabric charge . . $10.00
Private pants sewing instruction $20/ per hr.
Custom clients $60.00
    Additional muslin fabric charge . . $8.00
Custom clients (hip size over 46") . $75.00
    Additional muslin fabric charge . . $10.00
Fresh copy of
    original pants pattern $7.50

REDESIGNS FROM PANTS
BASIC PATTERN (my basic pattern)

Home-sewer (client provides
    copy of original $15.00
Custom clients $20.00
Design proofs in muslin $25.00
Four-piece, basic style (two fronts
    and two backs) .... $12.50-$15.00
Four-piece, trouser style (two fronts
    and two backs) .... $20.00-$25.00

CUSTOM TAILORED PANTS

Elastic waist pants without band . . $45.00
    With band $50.00
Unlined pants with waistband,
    fly front, darts $60.00
Lined pants with waistband,
    fly front, darts $65.00
Unlined trouser pants $75.00
Lined trouser pants $85.00
Jeans $75.00

Details and certain pockets an additional
charge based on difficulty

CUSTOM TAILORED PANTS
(Hip size over 46")

Elastic waist pants without a band . $55.00
    With band $60.00
Unlined pants with waistband,
    fly front, darts $65.00
Lined pants with waistband,
    fly front, darts $75.00
Unlined trouser pant $85.00
Lined trouser pant $95.00
Jeans $90.00

Details and certain pockets an additional
charge based on difficulty.

PRICES ARE APPROXIMATE (depending on fabric type and complexity) AND SUBJECT TO
CHANGE WITHOUT NOTICE.
PANTS PATTERNS ARE FULLY PAYABLE IN ADVANCE.
ALL FIT AND CONSTRUCTION FULLY GUARANTEED.

Effective 9/1/89

Design · Dressmaking · Instruction
1880 S.W. Heiney Road
Gresham, OR 97080
(503) 665-6505

CHAPTER 10

Alterations are Another Specialty

Specializing means **finding a need and filling it**. This phrase has meant success for many multi-million dollar businesses and it can for you too. The key is to target the need in your area and focus on filling it. Alterations may be that target.

I am delighted when a newcomer to dressmaking does all of the alterations she can handle. It is a tremendous learning experience. I know it sounds like boring work but consider the following questions. While you are building up a clientele and a profit base:

♦ *How much time will you spend educating an alterations customer?* **Not much.**

♦ *Are you responsible for an entire project?* **No.**

♦ *Will you satisfy a customer immediately with a tuck here and a hem there?* **Generally, yes.**

♦ *Will you get valuable training from working on many price levels of ready-made clothing and learning the tricks employed to speed up manufacturing?* **Yes!!**

♦ *Will you learn what you do and do not want to sew, or techniques you do or do not like?* **Yes.**

I predict you can make $30 per hour on alterations if you price right and work fast and efficiently. You should be able to hem two pair of lined pants in one hour (including fitting and delivery). If you charge $12 to $15 (depending on your market) per pair, you have just made $24 to $30 in one hour! You would only have to work three-plus hours to make $100 per day! Investing in a hemming machine and other speed equipment would allow you to do even more.

Yes, you will have to work fast. Slow dressmakers will definitely make less money (see Chapter 18 on working efficiently). Not every dressmaker, however, is as driven to reach the same financial goals that I am.

Where to Find Work

Remember, only 6% of America are active machine-sewers. The other 94% are your potential customers! Contact:

♦ Dry cleaners
♦ Ready-to-wear boutiques
♦ Department stores
♦ Hospitals and nursing homes (repairing sheets, pillowcases, towels, uniforms)
♦ Police and fire departments and other uniformed agencies
♦ School band and rally/cheerleader uniforms
♦ Uniform rental services.

Locate Private Alterations Clients

Let's say you decide you want to alter professional clothing — men's and women's business suits and women's tailored clothing. That's a great idea because these people **must** be well-dressed and so invest in expensive, quality clothing. They must also keep this investment in good condition. Initial alterations will generally have been done by the store where the clothing was purchased, but buttons fall off, skirt lengths change, zippers break, weight fluctuates. All require a dressmaker's careful attention.

You have "targeted your market." Now, how do you reach these people? Use your business cards or develop a flyer advertising your services. You can use my pants fitting flyer (see page 62) as a guide.

Look for concentrated sources of well-dressed people. Large corporations often have company bulletin boards or newsletters. Personnel departments frequently provide assistance with professional employee image development and could refer people to you. Large office buildings are similar to corporations, with cafeterias, bulletin boards and newsletters. Contact local image consultants and professional shoppers or wardrobe consultants. They are usually the first person a busy professional calls with a clothing distress signal.

Pricing Alterations

The absolutely best source of pricing information is Claire Shaeffer's book **Price It Right** (see page 121). Claire uses what she calls an "add-on unit system" formula. Since it is not a dollar amount, it can be used in any area, large city or small town, and is timeless.

CHAPTER 11

Advertising Your Services

My best advertising today comes from my satisfied customers. In addition to my high-quality work, I often do something special that I don't charge for: repairs, marking a hem, or giving a small handmade gift at delivery time. Their referrals keep me busy!

I found informal and word-of-mouth advertising to be the most cost-effective way to build my business. Consider doing the following:

◆ Place your business cards on community, church, school or office building bulletin boards.

◆ Make a special appointment to see the owner or manager of your local fabric shop; take in samples of your best work for her to see your quality. Leave several business cards or flyers so they can refer customers to you.

◆ Promote your skills by getting a part-time job in a fabric shop. I had several sales positions and earned money and received a shopping discount while I met many future clients. I also met people in the sewing industry, which has proved to be valuable long term.

◆ If you are interested in bridal, call local bridal shops and sell your alterations services. You will learn ready-to-wear techniques by working on ready-made gowns.

◆ Leave your business cards or make up a nice poster with a pocket on it to hold your cards in hair salons, especially for bridal and alterations.

Advertising in newspapers and in the Yellow Pages can be effective, but be sure to check advertising rates and get them in writing, as it can be expensive. Direct mail advertising by combining forces and sharing costs with a color consultant can be good business for both parties. The color consultant may become one of your best sources of new clients. She will meet many people whom she can refer to you as she does wardrobe clean-outs and color consultations, and you can suggest her services to clients who are in need of color analysis.

CHAPTER 12

Easy But Accurate Financial Records

Bank Accounts

It is important to have a separate business checking account for your new business. I have had my own account, no matter how small my balance might have been, for most of my business life. A business cannot function efficiently without its own checking account for easy record keeping.

When selecting a bank, take the time to do a market survey to find a bank with the best deal. Banks are like all other businesses and are becoming more competitive. Look for a bank that will not charge you additional fees if you have a $50 to $100 balance. You may even find a bank that is offering free checking with no minimum balance.

Be sure to ask your bank for an end-of-the-month statement date when you set up your account. This will make it easier to do your monthly book-keeping using my simple system. Otherwise, your statement will end at odd dates which will not coincide with your bookkeeping period.

If you use a business name, you will need a business checking account, which costs a bit more. Ask for "business deposit slips." They are larger and give you more room for a better, more detailed record of your deposits. Carbon checks are also handy. They save time and eliminate the possibility of forgetting to write the check amount in the check register.

Get to know the people at your bank, and make an effort to develop a relationship with a loan officer. As they watch your business grow, they may be willing to loan you money if you need to invest in new or additional equipment.

Bookkeeping

Have your tax specialist explain the different bookkeeping systems and help you set up a system that will be comfortable for you. You may find you like my easy system.

My Simple Bookkeeping System

I use the "**file and envelope system**," very common for small businesses. Buy 12 file folders and 24 8" × 10" manila envelopes. Label each file for a month of the year, and label one envelope **Expenses** and one envelope **Income** for each month. Place these in a file cabinet or box.

In each envelope marked **Expenses** I put all receipts for items purchased for the business, paid for by check or cash during that particular month. I try to write checks for everything. It makes bookkeeping cleaner and easier because I have a written document declaring my purchase. I always write on the check exactly what was purchased - sewing supplies or whatever. If I must pay cash, I ask for a cash receipt and list on it the name of the store, the date and the items purchased. I keep cash receipts clipped together inside the envelope.

In each monthly envelope marked **Income** I file all customer invoices from dressmaking, from classes I have taught, and any reimbursements due me from my other accounts for that month.

In each month's file folder I also place my balanced bank statement and my monthly bills for utilities that I will use at year end to figure my tax deductions for having a business in my home (see page 74). I file the telephone bill, heat, electricity, water and garbage bills here after they have been paid from my family checking account.

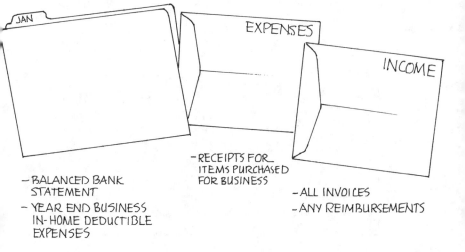

- BALANCED BANK STATEMENT
- YEAR END BUSINESS IN-HOME DEDUCTIBLE EXPENSES

- RECEIPTS FOR ITEMS PURCHASED FOR BUSINESS

- ALL INVOICES
- ANY REIMBURSEMENTS

At month end I add up each envelope and mark the totals on the outside. In the "Expense" envelope I make a list of items purchased by check and a separate list of items purchased with cash, then I total them separately.

Next I write a business check (I make this the last check of the month) to myself — from Kathleen Spike, KS Designs, to Kathleen Spike, person — for the total of the cash spent column. I am careful to note on the check what it is for: "Reimbursement for sewing supplies," for example.

NOTE: Since the cash spent was my personal cash, I pay that back to keep business and family money as separate as possible. If I were to spend $20 in cash every month on thread and supplies, that would be $240 per year that my family budget would be covering of my business expenses. I want my business to show a profit on its own, not because my family food budget is supporting it. Plus — business expenses are tax deductible — I don't want to lose track of them!

I now add "check expenses" and "cash expenses" for a grand total of "Expenses."

Next I total "income" and mark this total on the outside of the envelope. I also list the numbers of the invoices that are included in this month's income (#20 - #25, for example). That way I don't have to rummage through every envelope if I need to look up a past invoice.

I am always very careful to deposit **all** income checks in full. If I need money for **any** reason, I write a check out of the account for the expense. Do not ask for cash back on your business account deposits.

Now I have a total of my income and expenses for the month:

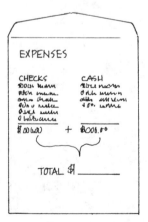

At the end of each month I take the information from my "file-and-envelope system" and transfer it to ledger sheets. I have two sheets for each month, one for each envelope. They have the same names as each envelope (**Expenses and Income**) but are used to show me exactly **where my income comes from and where I spent my money**. Buy ledger paper with enough columns so that you can divide your income into sections that make sense to you.

Columns I use on Ledger Sheets:

Income

1. Custom dressmaking
2. Sewing classes
3. Alterations
4. Tutoring
5. Pant design
6. Pant construction
7. Retail
8. Miscellaneous
9. Total

Expenses

1. Sewing supplies
2. Office expenses
3. Rents (outside class locations)
4. Printing
5. Professional organizations
6. Taxes and licenses
7. Maintenance (of my work space)
8. Contract labor
9. Equipment (purchase and repair)
10. Education (including magazines, books, etc.)
11. Improvements (to my work space)
12. Dry cleaning
13. Legal and professional fees
14. Travel expenses
15. Business entertainment
16. Bank charges
17. Deposits (to savings to pay taxes)
18. Total

Because my business has been in existence for some time, I have added several other sources of income to my basic dressmaking business. You can change columns any time you feel a need to track something new. I want to know exactly what is making money, so I create columns for everything. Your income ledger sheet may have only three columns: dressmaking, alterations, and miscellaneous. I really can't tell you which columns you should have because I don't know what you are doing in your business. Just remember that the **purpose of the income columns is to identify the source of your sales**.

The same thing is true of your "expense" columns. **The purpose of these columns is to keep track of the expenses you have, to tell you exactly where your money is going**. You can see from my expense columns that I spend my money in many different places. You might simply have the following expenses at the beginning:

1. Sewing supplies
2. Office expenses
3. Taxes and licenses
4. Maintenance

5. Dry cleaning
6. Legal and professional fees
7. Bank charges
8. Miscellaneous

How to Pay Yourself!

It is important to post (log in monies received and spent) on a monthly basis because the totals of these two sections tell you how much money you can pay yourself every month. AHA! Now I have your attention! When you have posted all items from each envelope onto the corresponding ledger sheet, total each column and then all columns on each sheet. Now — the difference between the totals columns on the "Income" sheet and the "Expense" sheet is your profit before taxes.

Income − expenses = profit before taxes

If you have an interest-bearing checking or savings account, don't forget to add that amount each month to your income sheet; in fact, you should have a column for interest if you receive it regularly. Also, your monthly checking account charge is an expense. (Note the column above called "bank charges.")

Don't pay yourself all of your "profit before taxes" from the above calculation. If you do, what will you do about expenses for the next month? Keep enough money in your checking account to cover the next month's estimated expenses and, based on your estimated tax computations, save money each month to pay your taxes. Then write yourself a check for the balance, for all of that hard but satisfying work you put in, and note on the check that it is "owner's draw." Your taxes are figured on the total "profit before taxes," not on what you pay yourself from this surplus.

Taxes

Sales Tax

In states that charge sales tax, you must collect and pay sales tax on items that you produce from **materials you provide,** or on items that you purchase for resale. The service you provide as a dressmaker working with **materials supplied by your client** is not taxable. This is important because you want to report only net sales so you don't pay sales tax on the sales tax when you fill out your monthly state sales tax report.

If you regularly sell taxable items, you might want to keep a separate "taxable sales income" envelope. To arrive at "net sales," subtract the total sales tax collected from invoices in this envelope.

Total invoices – total sales tax = net sales.

For your "income" ledger set up the sales tax entry as follows:

	Total Invoice Amount	– Sales Tax	NET SALES	Dressmaking	Alterations
Invoice #_____					
Invoice #_____					
Invoice #_____					

Sales tax then becomes a column on your "expense" ledger too.

Estimated Income Tax Payments

The IRS considers you to be self-employed if you are a sole proprietor or if you are in a business partnership. That means that you aren't being paid by an employer who is withholding tax money from your paycheck. That also means that you are responsible for estimating your income and making tax payments in advance. These estimated tax payments are due quarterly on January 15, April 15, June 15 and September 15. If you haven't paid 80% of the total tax you owe by the end of the year, the IRS can charge penalties. It is in your best interest to make these estimated tax payments. It is also easier to pay quarterly than to pay one larger lump at year end. If your state has income tax as well, you must pay that quarterly too.

Social Security (Self-Employment Tax)

You will also have to pay your own social security. If you were employed by another person your employer would pay part of your social security and the remainder would be deducted from your paycheck. Self-employed people pay the full amount themselves.

Home Office Deductions

One of the major advantages of working at home is that some home expenses not normally deductible on your income tax statement become deductible when you establish an office at home. Businesses that operate in outside space can deduct these costs, so it makes sense that the home-based business should be able to do this too. What it means to you is that your business is not only providing income for you and your family, but is also helping to defray some costs that you would be paying anyway.

As a wise friend once said, "Deducting something doesn't make it free, it just makes what you wanted to do anyway cost less." Remember that thought. Here are some possible home office deductions. Be sure to talk to your tax specialist about which will apply to you and what records you must keep to back up the deduction.

The biggest deductions:

♦ Rent

♦ Mortgage interest

♦ Depreciation

♦ Real estate taxes

Smaller ones add up too:

♦ Cleaning

♦ Lights

♦ Heating

♦ Home repairs related to business

♦ Household supplies

♦ Insurance premiums

♦ Telephone

♦ Trash collections

♦ Water

♦ Landscaping and lawn care
(if clients come to your home)

I suggest you order a booklet from the IRS called "Business Use of Your Home," publication 3587 (See page 120). It is well worth reading. It will answer a lot of your questions and help you communicate better with your tax specialist.

Standard Business Deductions

Regular business deductions are expenses of operating your business, whether it is home-based or outside. It is important to know what these items are from the beginning so that you can carefully save receipts for purchases to document them as business expenses. It is always best to pay for these items with a business check.

Deductible Expenses

(In addition to those listed above)

- Accounting/tax preparation
- Advertising and promotion
- Bank service charges
- Books and periodicals (promotional magazines, newspapers, newsletters)
- Car expenses or mileage
- Consulting and other services
- Conventions and conferences of business and trade organizations
- Dues to professional and trade associations
- Education and professional development (classes, travel)
- Entertainment (partial deduction)
- Food while traveling (partial deduction)
- Furniture and equipment
- Gifts to current or future clients or business associates (maximum per year - $25/person)
- Insurance premiums
- Interest on business loans
- Legal fees
- License fees and taxes
- Local transportation
- Office supplies
- Postage and shipping
- Printing and duplicating
- Repairs and maintenance on business equipment
- Telephone
- Tips
- Transportation and out-of-town travel expenses
- Wages

Family Employees

I think it is important to learn to do your own bookkeeping before you hire someone else to do it for you. This does not apply to tax work, as I always have that done by a professional. In the beginning I alone used my "file-and-envelope" system and ledger sheets. When my daughter turned 13, I taught her to do the posting and balancing. She wanted to work for me and I liked the quality of her work. She still works for me and sometimes she works on the books in the studio while I sew. She earns a salary, does wonderful work, and we have a great sense of togetherness.

My son also works for me in the maintenance and janitorial division. He keeps my studio orderly and keeps my equipment cleaned, oiled and in good working condition. He sweeps the entry, does the yard work and all the heavy lifting and rearranging. It took him until age 15 to decide he was willing work for Mom, but he finally saw the light!

Family members are the most logical people to hire. This keeps the money within your family and there are some tax benefits too (ask your tax specialist). I have no conflicts with my children about working for me. We have rather strict rules and consequences if the children do not do their work. They receive two warnings, but if they still do not complete their work, $20 is automatically deducted from their paycheck at the end of the month. The older they get the more reliable they are becoming. Quite simply, they want the money!

Computers

A computer is a wonderful tool for the individual business owner — saving you hours of record-keeping time once you learn how to use it. There are programs available for under $100 that can write checks, balance your checkbook and track expenses all at the same time. Check your local computer store.

Other programs are available for word processing (much more fun than a typewriter!), project management, and inventory control. Spreadsheets can let you play with different pricing combinations or hourly rates, automatically re-calculating totals when you change one of the other numbers in the formula. Word processing and desktop publishing programs allow you to create professional-looking price lists, forms and flyers without the expense of typesetting. Explore the possibilities if you (or other members of your family) are interested.

Tips for Good Money Management

♦ Remember to leave money in your business checking account for "overhead" expenses — it is painful to have to put money back in once you have drawn it out as "earnings."
♦ If you find you have more than $1000 sitting in your business acount from one month to the next (for quarterly tax payments or other larger occasional expenses), open an interest-bearing checking account.
♦ Establish a time each day, week, month and quarter to take care of record-keeping, timekeeping, billing, bill paying and banking. Sometimes it can help to have a calendar to follow, especially to remind you of quarterly tax payments.
♦ Keep all your business records together in one area, separate from your personal records.
♦ Manage your sewing notions inventory — don't get caught short. Keep lists of what you need. Record when you use or add to your supply. With good cost records you can make sure you aren't losing money by not charging your clients enough to cover costs.

CHAPTER 13

Client Records - Good Ones Make Business Easier

Establishing a group of on-going clients has made life easier for me. New customers take more time because we take time to get to know each other. I must learn my client's clothing preferences, fitting differences and lifestyle. I will often draft basic patterns for her and then re-use them frequently. My client must learn my work, and that my famly comes first for me — especially in an emergency!

I spend a lot of time educating my customers in line and design, fashion, color and wardrobe planning so that we are working together in the most productive and rewarding manner. One of my greatest responsibilities to me and to my client is to ask questions and record the responses **once** so we can both maximize our time. To help myself do this, I have created forms that are good organizers and timesavers for me.

Please Copy My Forms

Because I know how many years of experience and hours of time it has taken me to create and refine the forms I use, I want to save you that time and effort. In this chapter I have included a small copy of each form so you can see what it looks like and how I use it. In the back of the book I have added full-page forms for you to remove and reproduce.

Carefully remove the forms with a razor blade and take them to a quick printer. Ask the printer to increase the size 200%, typeset and paste on your business information over the top of mine, and print it for you. This would cost me $7 for the one-time typeset charge and about $5.50 for 100 printed copies of black ink on white 20-pound paper. Call several print shops to price compare; prices vary wildly! You can also type or neatly print in your information, enlarge the form 200% on an enlarging copy machine and then make copies, but the quality may not be as good.

"The Lady"

For each new client on her first visit I fill out a complete measurement chart that I call "**The Lady**," and I begin the client's personal file. (See page 125 for reproducible form.) One year later I take her measurements again. Even though her weight may not have changed one pound, it is amazing how fast bodies can change shape. The Palmer/Pletsch book **Clothes Sense** will give you more information on figure type. (See page 124.)

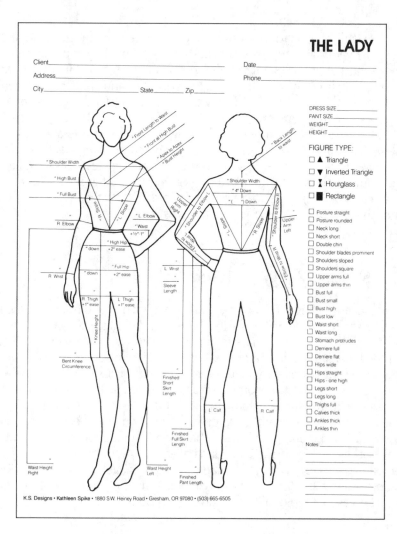

THE LADY

Client_____ Date_____
Address_____ Phone_____
City_____ State_____ Zip_____

DRESS SIZE_____
PANT SIZE_____
WEIGHT_____
HEIGHT_____

FIGURE TYPE:

☐ ▲ Triangle
☐ ▼ Inverted Triangle
☐ ✗ Hourglass
☐ ■ Rectangle

☐ Posture straight
☐ Posture rounded
☐ Neck long
☐ Neck short
☐ Double chin
☐ Shoulder blades prominent
☐ Shoulders sloped
☐ Shoulders square
☐ Upper arms full
☐ Upper arms thin
☐ Bust full
☐ Bust small
☐ Bust high
☐ Bust low
☐ Waist short
☐ Waist long
☐ Stomach protrudes
☐ Derriere full
☐ Derriere flat
☐ Hips wide
☐ Hips straight
☐ Hips - one high
☐ Legs short
☐ Legs long
☐ Thighs full
☐ Calves thick
☐ Ankles thick
☐ Ankles thin

Notes:_____
_____
_____
_____
_____

K.S. Designs • Kathleen Spike • 1880 S.W. Heiney Road • Gresham, OR 97080 • (503) 665-6505

The Work Agreement

After I have measured her, the client and I discuss her project and I fill in the **Work Agreement** (see page 126). I use NCR (no carbon required) two-part paper so that I am making a duplicate for my client as I write. NCR paper is more expensive than using carbon paper but it is so much easier and tidier. To me it is worth the price. My client and I sign the Work Agreement and then each keep a copy. This is a valid contract between the two of us.

I then use this work agreement during the garment construction process to log my time and additional costs. When it is time to figure my bill, the Work Agreement is my time card. I simply transfer this information in an understandable form to my invoice. After billing, the Work Agreement goes into the client's file with her other paperwork as a swatched and accurate reminder of this garment. I have my client's closet in a file folder!

A very important part of this Work Agreement is logging my time in and time out. This is how I establish the time it takes for any garment to travel through my business. I use this information to figure my base price and the garment prices on my price list.

When it is time to re-evaluate my pricing, I simply pull all of my Work Agreements dated from the last price change and compare the time it takes to sew a specific type of garment now, compared to then. Prices may go up or down to reflect that change. If I have developed a new technique that makes blouse-sewing go faster, I will see that trend from my time notations and my price may go down. Or I may decide to keep the price the same and thus increase my profitability. (Changes in hourly rates are a separate matter.)

The Evaluation Form

I have an evaluation form to fill out after each garment is completed. Some clients will do this and some will not, but I look forward to having a record of satisfaction, or constructive criticism to know how I am doing. How can I improve if I don't know how I am doing? How can I feel a sense of pride and accomplishment if my client doesn't tell me? (See page 127).

KS

YOUR COMMENTS, PLEASE

for
**KATHLEEN
SPIKE**

Date_____

Please help me keep you a satisfied customer. Complete this evaluation and return it to me so I can serve you better another time.

PROJECT_____

FOR_____

	Very Satisfactory	Acceptable	Unsatisfactory
GENERAL APPEARANCE Comments:			
FIT Comments:			
DETAILS Comments:			
Other Comments:			

Thank you for your cooperation.

_____

KS Designs

Design • Dressmaking • Instruction
1880 S.W. Heiney Road
Gresham, OR 97080
(503) 665-6505

Client Files

Each client's file, filed alphabetically, contains her **"Lady"** and copies of all past work orders. This way I have an accurate swatched record of every item I have sewn for that client. Any correspondence is also included, as well as completed evaluation forms. I also include any notes that I make during meetings so I can remember the details. This is my response to having my mind overfilled with facts — if I write them down and file them, I don't have to remember them any longer!

Invoices

When I first started handing out invoices, I used standard blank receipt forms available in office supply stores. Now I have 5½" × 8½" 3-part NCR forms custom-printed with my logo and address. (NCR paper does not require messy carbons.) Even when handwritten, they look professional. With three copies I can give one to my client, put one in the client's file, and put the third in my bookkeeping records in my monthly Income envelope.

CHAPTER 14

Business Guidelines

I encourage you to begin your business with a set of written guidelines (I call mine **My Business and Service Style**). They can be changed and improved any time as you grow and change. Written guidelines can eliminate potential misunderstandings between you and your client, and they set a businesslike attitude. Another positive result of printed guidelines is discussing work style in advance, rather than after a problem arises.

My purpose for creating the guidelines was to get control over my rapidly growing business. I came to the point where I could not remember what I had told to whom, so I committed everything to paper.

I mail my price list and guidelines to a potential client before the first consultation. They appreciate this advance information. My guidelines give them something tangible to use to evaluate my business and they showcase me as a professional. My price list gives the client a chance to see in advance what kind of financial investment they will be making. It is also a good idea to frame and post your guidelines by the mirror in your fitting area so the client can re-read them while you are fitting her.

My Personal Rules

I have some unwritten rules that are just for me:

1. If I think a client's requests or choices are going to make the garment unattractive, I tell them so in a diplomatic way. This communication brings sanity to my work (see pages 87-88).

2. If I have begun a project and I see a design change that is pertinent to the overall look of the garment, I will discuss it with the client over the phone. If it means that I cannot finish the garment today because I cannot reach the client, I will move on to another project. I never continue sewing if I have a question. If I do, I become totally responsible for the results. If I know I am right, I make the decision and accept responsibility for it.

3. I never charge the customer for what I don't know how to do. This is not to say that I have never winged it and come out on top! For example, if I don't know how to fit pants but I know how to sew them, I will charge for the construction time and count the fitting as experience. I make this agreement with the client before I take on the project. It is completely acceptable for you to tell a client that you are not familiar with a technique, but you want to learn. She can only respect your openness and eagerness to learn. Be cautious though. It is better to say no than to do a poor job.

4. I feel it is my responsibility to stand behind all of my work. If I ruin a design, then I am obligated to replace that fabric, even if I do not finish the project. I want to have an attitude of service in my business.

5. Occasionally I have a client who questions my prices. It is up to me to decide whether my rates fairly reflect the market, and my skills and experience. I stand firm on my fees. I will agree with the client: "You are absolutely right, it is an expensive service to have a piece of clothing made especially for you." What can she say? I have agreed with her in a kind and honest manner. It is now her choice to spend the money or not.

Guidelines Promote Professionalism

A woman working in the home can give the appearance of not seriously being in business. A client may think that her work is not worth very much. It is up to you and how you present your business to determine whether this is true for you. When I committed my guidelines to paper, I felt my business became more important, and I am sure my attitude toward my clients reflected this too.

I am a member of the **Custom Clothing Guide of Oregon** (see page 120). It is a trade organization whose main purpose is to provide networking, education and promotion for its custom clothing business members. This group is helping to establish guidelines for dressmakers in our area.

I have printed my business guidelines for you to read. This is not for you to reproduce like the forms in Chapter 13, but to help you decide what is important for you. Please feel free to use my format and my words if you must, but it is extremely important that **your** guidelines reflect **your** feelings and thoughts.

My Business and Service Style

I am pleased that you have chosen to have me create a custom garment. This is a unique service and I would like to take this opportunity to share my procedures and style of service with you.

Turnaround Time

It takes approximately six to eight weeks from initial consultation to delivery of your completed garment. Unforeseen complications in design changes, fittings, the search for "just the right fabric and findings," and family needs may affect the delivery date. Long-time clients will have a shorter turnaround time as fewer decisions need to be made on each project. Rushing in the planning stages can lead to poor choices. Each client is important to me and receives every consideration that I can give.

Fitting Appointments

Please be on time for all appointments (or call), wear suitable lingerie and either wear or bring the correct shoes. Due to the importance of proper foundations in fitting, I will **not** fit you without them. An additional $20 fitting fee will be charged and a new session scheduled.

I will notify you if it becomes necessary to change an appointment, and it would please me if you would do the same. Call or leave a message on my answering machine.

Fees

My price sheet explains set fees for specific garments. Other fees will be estimated. Prices include consultations, phone calls, design planning and changes, fabric preparation, precutting the paper pattern, cutting out garment, sewing, fitting, pressing, and final delivery/billing. Basic pant designs are fully payable in advance. Other garments require a 25% deposit and full payment upon delivery. A $20 deposit for findings will be due at our first appointment.

Patterns

I have accumulated an extensive collection of fine patterns in a range of sizes from which you may select, or you may purchase your own pattern. Although the final choice will be yours, selecting the right pattern and fabric to create the desired effect is the very essence of my role in consulting on each project. I have experienced custom clients who know their wardrobe needs, their figure, their color personalities and also know fabric and design. They may feel comfortable making these decisions unaided. However, collaborating can bring new ideas that make the whole process a lot of fun. By working together we can make design and size changes that we never would have thought of alone. I can also help you formulate a wardrobe plan and an overall color scheme.

Fabrics

An investment wardrobe deserves to be constructed of the best fabric you can afford. Natural fibers or superior quality synthetics will be your best in fabric choices. Your job will be to purchase the ultimate choice and mine is to pretreat the fabric and purchase the necessary findings (findings are added to the price of the custom project).

A lot of thought and consideration goes into each new client's project. Since I specialize in investment clothing, the garments we create should work in your wardrobe for many years. I will become acquainted with each of you, getting to know your lifestyle and clothing needs. This enables me to better guide you.

I look forward to working with you.

Respectfully,

Kathleen Spike
1880 SW Heiney Rd.
Gresham, OR 97030
(503) 665-6505

CHAPTER 15

Develop Good Client Relationships

Communication and Decision-Making

Communicating with clients is challenging and enjoyable. When we all speak English we **think** we understand each other. I have discovered that's not always the case. It takes a great deal of tact to communicate with clients about their clothing. It is important to remember that a person's self-image is involved when you work with hair or clothing, because that is how the client perceives herself and is perceived by the outside world.

As a dressmaker, it is your responsibility to set your client at ease and to lead the conversation. People are shy about asking a dressmaker the right questions, such as "May I see a sample of your work?" or "How much do you charge?" You must provide your client with these answers even though she may not have the courage to ask. By sending out my price list and "My Business and Service Style," I have answered many questions before my client arrives.

It is important to use techniques that involve the client in the decision-making process. You may think the client is hearing and understanding you, but often she is not. This is another good reason for my "Work Agreement" that spells out our decisions on paper. You may have a client who will say, "Oh, you make all of the decisions, everything you do is so wonderful." Beware of that approach and don't allow a client to flatter you into taking on the responsibility for all of the decisions. It is important that she become involved in developing her own clothing. She will learn and grow if she shares in creating a garment and will become a more confident and knowledgeable customer.

I use many techniques to involve my clients. If I am looking at a skirt that has too much design ease and I think we should eliminate some, I pull the skirt to the back in an exaggerated position and then release it. This way she can really see my point about less ease. This also gets her physically and mentally involved with the decision. If we feel, touch, hear and see, we are more likely to understand.

Learning to Communicate

When I first started my business I made some big mistakes but I learned from each one of them. I want to share a "then" and a "now" situation with you to help you see the importance of good communication. The way I progressed from "then" to "now" was to study and to practice effective communication. There is some homework that you can do too. Read the books in my Bibliography under "Psychology and Communications," page 120. They helped me to establish a plan for my personal and business life and helped me see the power I have to direct my own life — and they can help you too.

My "Then" Story

Very early on, I failed in communicating with a new client. She called and said she was referred by another client. "I have a pattern and fabric and want to know if you can sew it for me right away?" I said yes. The new client arrived with a poor quality fabric and an inappropriate pattern. I was uncomfortable with all of it from first glance. The client wasn't sure about it either. She had purchased the dream of looking like the model in the pattern catalog. She had no concept of what shapes, colors or designs would look best on her.

I am embarrassed to say I took the job because I needed the money. I **didn't** say that inexpensive fabric will always look inexpensive, no matter how beautiful the workmanship. I **didn't** say the garment will not turn out like the picture in the pattern book.

The first fitting took place and the fabric and design lines were not cooperating. The client had gained five pounds since she was first measured but she assured me she was going to lose the weight. She insisted I fit the dress tightly to her former measurements. I complied even though this little voice inside me kept telling me this was a mistake. I was not confident enough to enforce what I knew to be correct about fit. The client decided to have only one fitting because she was rushed, and I was too meek to insist on more.

The delivery date arrived. The client came to pick up the dress and was thrilled with the bill because she had a dress for only $35. I didn't tell her it took ten hours and many gray hairs. The client left happy, but I was exhausted and confused. I loved my business, but why did I feel so used and that I had not made a profit?

The next week the client phoned and told me the dress was too tight in the waist. I suggested she come over and I would look at it. I spent three more hours trying to get the wrong fabric, the wrong style and too tight of a fit to work for the client and her figure. We finally came to an agreement and again the client left happy. I was miserable because I felt used again. I did not have the courage to be honest with the client.

In looking back, I can now see that we did not share in the decision-making process, the client did it all. I was not in charge; I did not speak my mind; I did not give the client the benefit of my experience.

"Now" Has a Happy Ending!

A potential client calls, telling me she has fabric and pattern and wants a dress made. I explain that I would like to see both before accepting the job. I also explain that there is a $25 consultation fee that will be waived if I decide to take the project. I mention I will be sending my price and work style information sheets (see pages 56 & 84) through the mail. This saves us both time and gives the client an idea of how much I charge and how my business functions.

When the client arrives for her appointment, I greet her and we look at her fabric and pattern. I take a few quick measurements and observe her posture and overall figure type. We discuss her lifestyle and her clothing requirements. The client responds to my questions about the types of clothing she is most comfortable wearing and the fabrics that make her feel good. I ask her if she knows her "style." I want to know if she has a plan for her wardrobe. Does everything marry together - accessories, colors, textures? We will have a lot of preliminary work to do if she does not have the answers to my questions. I mention that I charge $20 per hour to research and define a long-range wardrobe plan.

At this time the client may choose to pay the $25 consultation fee and not use my wardrobe planning or sewing services. Or we may dive right in and go to work. Occasionally a client will ponder my words and call back several months later.

Let's assume we are going to proceed. I tell the client that this style may not be successful on her figure and point out why. I make sure I never criticize her choice, just that I point out how wrong it would be of me not to share what I know about flattering lines and body types. Generally, the client is thankful that I have recognized this and she has only invested the the price of the pattern.

The next topic is the fabric. I tell her that the color and design are beautiful (again not criticizing her choice) but the type of the fabric will disappoint her in the design she has selected. It will cling to her figure and the seams will pucker because she has chosen a hard-finished, tightly woven synthetic. I cannot work with this fabric and charge the prices that I feel my skills demand. My conscience would not let me. Also, to work on lower quality fabrics, I would have to charge about half of what I am charging today. I have made a choice to upgrade my skills and to specialize in high quality fabrics which are generally more expensive. My skills command a higher hourly charge, and I love working on fabulous fabrics. Whenever I sew for a client she must purchase the best quality fabric she can afford, so she will get the best value from my service

The client is grateful for my helping her avoid a wardrobe mistake. She is pleased to be learning and wants me to help her select a dress fabric that is worth my time and her money. I am happy because I have been honest and straightforward about what works best for me.

I find that my clients and I are both happier when I assert myself and speak openly, when I share my professional opinion and experience with them, and when we make decisions together that work for both of us.

We dressmakers must become as knowledgeable as we can in fit, color, fabrics, figure analysis, current sewing techniques and design. We must never stop studying and learning our changing craft. We also must become masters of communication, the psychology of client relations, and business. We must be confident in our knowledge and use it to guide our clients to good choices.

Good Telephone Communication Can Save Time

As you can see from the above stories, I have learned to communicate better with potential clients by taking time with them to explain my work style, pricing, construction and design techniques and deadlines. This initial conversation can also give me an idea of what this potential client may be like and whether I want to work with her. I listen to the speaker's tone of voice, choice of words, knowledge of her wardrobe and her figure, and her attitudes toward dressmakers.

You should be the one in charge of the conversation. Learn what questions are valuable for you to ask a potential client. I occasionally receive calls in which a caller asks, "Are you the lady who sews?" or "Are you the seamstress?" I respond, "Yes, I operate a custom clothing business and I am a dressmaker. How may I help you?"

Please use proper terminology when referring to your profession. It will enhance your image as a professional and it will increase the general public awareness of the importance of dressmaking and custom clothing businesses. You may call yourself a designer, sewing professional, tailor, textile specialist, wardrobe planner, or whatever you feel your expertise may be. Choose, and then teach your family, friends, associates and clients to use your correct title.

Ask These Questions

The next question I hear is, "I have some fabric and a pattern and I would like to know if you can make it up for me?" I respond by saying, "First, I must ask you some questions to see if I am the right dressmaker for you." I work to set her at ease with the tone of my voice and straightforward manner. Here are some of the questions I ask:

1. Have you worked with a dressmaker previously?
2. What size do you usually wear in a ready-to-wear?
3. Would you say your weight is average for your height?
4. What is your work environment?
5. Are you hoping that this dress will cost you less than you would pay in the store for a similar dress?
6. What is the fiber content of the fabric if you have already purchased it? Have you looked at patterns yet? If so, which ones did you like, what are the numbers? (I have pattern books in my studio for reference. I can usually buy the last month's books for a small fee from a fabric store.)
7. What kind of a time factor are we talking about? Is this to be done for a special occasion with a specific date?

As we talk I get a feel for whether I want to continue with this client or not. It is important to develop the ability to screen the clients who share your sense of quality and commitment to good clothing, and refer others to a more compatible dressmaker for them. As you become more experienced you will be better able to make educated guesses about this potential client. Work smart! Dressmaking is a very personal service and it has a high potential for failure if the personalities don't mesh. Keep telling yourself:

I HAVE A RIGHT TO ASK ALL OF THESE (ABOVE) QUESTIONS.

I HAVE A RIGHT TO CHOOSE MY CLIENTS.

I HAVE THE RIGHT TO SAY NO!

CHAPTER 16

A Sample Project From Start to Finish

I felt it would be valuable for you to follow the development of a client's project. Let's assume this is a new client and we have had our initial consultation (see pages 87-89). She is bringing fabric for approval.

Before the client's arrival I have gathered a tape measure, *The Lady* chart, and my appointment and work order books. All are placed in the client reception area of my studio. I have also laid out pattern books and fashion magazines for inspiration.

The client arrives, we shake hands, I invite her to be seated. I ask her **again** if she has any questions about my printed materials. Most clients do not really absorb my information, but my guidelines are there in black and white. Most misunderstandings are covered by the statements in "My Business and Service Style" sheet. When a client questions me I might say, "I am sorry you misunderstood. I put these ideas on paper to free up my mind to concentrate on your design and sewing. I am excited about what we are working on. Do you think we can continue working together?"

The Fun Begins

Now we come to the rewarding part — creating beautiful clothes. I examine her fabric choices. I am looking for a long-wearing, quality fabric that will not create sewing problems, and that is appropriate for creating the final beautiful garment. I also want to make sure the fabric warrants the prices I charge.

We talk about her wardrobe plan: is this the color and style we discussed at our consultation? Does she have a date when the garment must be completed? This question often determines whether I can take a project, as I work to accommodate clients' deadlines.

As the client and I talk I do a mental evaluation:
♦ Do I really feel comfortable with this person?
♦ Are we speaking a similar language?

◆ Do I think she will be fun to work with? This is important!

◆ Will I see her again after the initial project, which always takes much more time?

◆ Do I like her style of dress, and do I want to (and can I) work with her figure?

I feel quite comfortable with our sample client and am willing to take a chance with her. I never know at first if I will be successful with a client. I can only make an educated guess.

Taking Measurements

Some clients are very modest and others just throw off their clothes anywhere, so it is important to have window coverings or privacy of some kind. Measuring gives me time to study the client's figure. I take careful measurements and make specific notes of the things that numbers will not show, such as a high hip. I am thoughtful and quiet as I measure so that I can be accurate with my numbers, description and mental picture of her body.

While measuring I give specific directions to the client to help her stand and move. Clients are often nervous, so I do my best to put them at ease and to give clear instructions. Be firm with your touch and directions; it helps create security for the client and greater confidence in your abilities.

I talk to my client about what I am doing and what is coming next. It helps her to relax if I provide a verbal roadmap. If the client asks about the numbers, I suggest we review them later. I say, "Now remember, these are not beauty contest measurements, they are clothing measurements. I am giving you ease in each measurement so you can move in your clothes." It is my goal to help every client, no matter what her size or shape, to feel good about her body.

When we review the measurements, I do not tell the client what pattern size she will wear. I tell her I need to analyze everything, and I will purchase the pattern and add it to her bill. Clients who are accustomed to buying better ready-to-wear may purchase a size 6 dress and become quite upset when they discover they wear a size 10 pattern. I explain that retail sizing is not consistent. "Vanity sizing" means the more you pay, the smaller the size. Personally, I can wear a size 4 in Anne Klein, a size 14 at K-Mart, but I always wear a size 10 pattern. Only patterns are consistent. **And the important thing is for the finished garment to fit well.**

Creating the Design Plan

We discuss the client's figure type, where she varies from "average," and how this affects the design we chose. I use as many commercial patterns, or parts of them, as I can. This saves my client money, as I charge $20 per hour for design work. We create a "design plan" that combines the client's figure type with her personal style.

My client wants a jacket and skirt and has purchased a lovely Italian wool based upon my recommendations from our consultation. She is a "romantic and feminine" style so our choice is a curvy jacket with pretty piping, cut just above her fullest hip point. She is slim-hipped, so this length is flattering. A fitted straight skirt with a slit completes the suit.

This client is a former home-sewer who is now too busy to sew. Even though she loves it, her full-time job and busy social life prevent her from sewing for herself. She wants to continue to make some easier items, but she values quality construction and fit and cannot devote the time required to produce finely tailored clothing. This is one reason why dressmaking is booming today. I don't ever want my clients to think I have to make everything they wear. (My daughter says, "Mom, if you make all of my clothes then I can't ever go shopping!")

We schedule the first fitting, she is on her way and I am back to work. I keep my appointments to 30-45 minutes. This time is factored into my base price for the garment.

Preparing the Fabric

I pretreat the fabric by washing or dry cleaning and charge the client. If the garment is to be washed, I wash and press the fabric for $1 per yard. I made a deal with my dry cleaner to charge $1 per yard to dry clean and press my fabric. I pretreat all fabrics for one reason: protection for my business. If there is going to be a problem with the fabric (dye can run, finishes can be removed and change the character of the fabric, shrinkage can take place), I want to know before I make up the garment.

It is important to develop a good working relationship with your dry cleaner. Ask for a tour of their facility so you can understand their process. A responsible dry cleaner will respect you as a professional and valuable customer, and will work to assist you. Keep looking until you find a responsive one.

Cutting the Garment

The day before I cut, I make a list of garments ready for cutting. This is determined by fitting and delivery dates. The night before, I go over the sequence for the cut day in my mind. I am up by 5:30am and cutting by 7:00 because I am freshest in the early morning. When I begin I know exactly what to do for maximum efficiency because I have organized my things and thoughts the day before.

The efficient layout of my cutting room (see page 41) helps me to make the best use of my time. If I have planned well, I will have everything I need for cutting. It wastes time and money when I have to go back to a project for further cutting. I will cut the fashion fabric, lining, interfacing and do all marking and alterations at one time.

After cutting, each project goes into a bin. I use resealable plastic bags to hold small items. The project now waits until one to three days before the first fitting appointment (or perhaps just hours!) when I am ready to baste up the garment.

First Fitting

I make appointments as early as 6:00am, preferring daytime or Saturdays. I have an occasional evening appointment, but I do not schedule them during my family dinner time. Also, everyone is tired after a full day of work. My clients are swollen from a day of eating and they do not concentrate as well.

When the client arrives for her fitting, I have her garment hanging in a visible place. I have advised her to wear appropriate lingerie and shoes. Without them we will not have the fitting, though she will be billed for the time as scheduled. Some clients resist accepting responsibility for the fitting process. I believe they simply do not understand the importance of proper undergarments and shoes. I gently but firmly inform them about this charge as it appears on "My Business and Service Style" sheet.

We discuss design changes, technique possibilities and finishing details. We schedule our next meeting and again have spent 30-45 minutes. Are you surprised at how short my appointments are? I develop a camaraderie with my clients, but have had to learn how to end a conversation gracefully. I can't afford to lose an entire morning of work by chatting. I develop a real love for my clients and they for me. We learn about and care about each others' families and jobs. We share personal time, but we never abuse the privilege. We respect each others' time. I have created this positive atmosphere in my business and you can do it too.

Completing the Garment

I correct the baste, only occasionally taking it completely apart and restitching the entire garment. I strive for minor adjustments through good preliminary planning, doing a muslin prototype if necessary, and selecting the right shape for the client's figure. If necessary we schedule one more fitting at which all is finalized and only hand stitching remains. (I do not like taking apart a finished garment!) The garment is now ready for final delivery.

Delivery time! I am excited — I have completed a project and will receive my reward, a check. When the client arrives, the studio is in order and I am well-dressed, calm and happy. It is easier to give money to a cheerful person!

I proudly display her suit. I found that if I am visibly pleased with the garment, the client is more likely to be too. She tries on the garment for final approval. If she changes her mind later, it is at her expense. Once approved, we talk about the next project, then I hand her the bill. Some clients look at the total and write a check, while others study all of the charges. I wait quietly and confidently. If the client has a question, I answer by pointing to the amount. Because money conversations can make people uncomfortable, I make it a habit not to verbalize the dollar amount.

Getting Paid

My client is giving her money directly to me — a very personal exchange. I am grateful for the payment and say "Thank you" several times, especially as the client walks out the door. I say, "I appreciate your business so much, I hope we can work together again. Thank you." I *never* say, "Thank you for the money," or "Thank you for the check." I want to keep the exchange impersonal.

I never allow a garment to leave my studio unpaid. In seventeen years I have had only one bad check and the client is still with me. This is a very wealthy woman who went on a trip and accidentally overdrew her account. Six weeks later she brought me cash because she felt so badly. My clients are very trustworthy and conscientious. I do not take credit cards. If I did, I would add the service charge to each charge invoice and note this on my price sheet.

What If...

Occasionally a client comes to pick up her garment and during the final try-on finds something that is wrong. I jump right in to solve the problem. If time allows, I seat her with a magazine, then fit and sew until the garment is right. Fit problems in the final garment mean I was not paying attention during earlier fittings.

If there is a problem with the finished garment, I do not internalize these mistakes. I have simply made an error, I am not a bad person nor a bad dressmaker. Dressmakers have a history of trying to perform magic — turning lumps and bumps into sleek beauty. I maintain a good attitude and my clients are understanding and willing to learn with me. If not, I choose not to work for them.

Some other "what if's":

♦ If a client does not like the final presentation and wants to make a design change, that is her choice but she is charged for changes at this stage.

♦ If there is a fit problem, it is my responsibility to correct it at my expense as I did not see it during the fittings.

♦ If this is an overly picky client who won't be happy even if the garment is perfect, I must make a decision. Do I want to please this person so I can keep her as a client, or do I want to fix the problem as best I can and hope I never see her again? There are some people who will never be happy with anything you or I make for them; we must accept that.

My goal is to take lemons and make lemonade. I want to make my client happy and confident in me. A designer garment is corrected many times before it is produced in quantity. Remind your clients that they are getting something even better — a one-of-a-kind original — and there is more room for error because of its uniqueness.

I have occasionally made a garment that the client loved but I did not. It is important to evaluate and learn from this. I have said, "I understand you like this style; next time I want to suggest a new shape that may be even more flattering to your figure." Clients continue to change. Many a conservative client has turned into a dramatic dresser with a little fashion direction. I work to increase my clients' fashion awareness and acceptance. My love and expertise is **fashion** dressmaking.

CHAPTER 17

Fashion for You and Your Clients

How do **you** dress? Are you as stylish as your budget and time permit? Are you up on current color and fashion trends? Fashion awareness is a big factor in my success, especially with my business focusing on quality fibers, wardrobe plans and fine detailing. I must dress for my success.

In the business world we have one opportunity to make a favorable first impression. If a client has not already seen your handiwork worn by someone else, she will judge your abilities by the way you dress and present yourself. Dressmaking requires a tremendous amount of trust from your client. To gain this trust, dress slightly above the market you are working to reach. Be sure you are adequately expressing your level of taste and professionalism. Fifty percent of my business results from being a role model for students and custom clients. I have made many garments for clients that are copies of what I was wearing that day.

Even when I am sewing at home with no appointments, I put on a well-planned casual outfit (loose-fitting pants and top for comfort and easy moving) with accessories. I never know who will drop in or when a client will call with a change in schedule. Plus, I like to look my best for myself and my family. For fittings and consultations I wear tailored pants with a more business-like sweater or blouse, or a jumpsuit. I keep in mind that my clients' opinion of me is created by my professional appearance and my tidy studio.

Do Your Fashion and Sewing Homework

I keep the walls in my studio covered with clippings from fashion magazines. They inspire me and develop my eye for current trends. I choose the shapes most valuable to my clients and to me.

The magazine I find most valuable is "W" (see page 123). It is a bit fashion forward for my taste, but it has much to offer in seasonal trends and fashion direction.

When I go through magazines, I look for an item like a new accessory, circle it on each page, and by the end of the magazine will see a trend developing. It is important for me to know fashion direction, as my clients depend on me for advice. I also have a great clipping service — my husband! He never misses a fashion article in the newspaper and saves them all for me.

It is important to keep abreast of what is happening in the fashion sewing world. I am an avid reader of sewing publications and I use them for reference, inspiration and self-education. I use the public library too. I take several sewing periodicals and consider these essential in keeping current in my field. These subscriptions are tax deductible. I take *Sew News, Threads, McCall Patterns Magazine,* and *Vogue Patterns* magazine.

Your business will improve if you become curious about every bit of information available in the sewing and textile field.

Figures and Fashion

With every shift in fashion there are new silhouettes that each client can wear. Unless I make a muslin prototype, I can never be sure how a new shape will look on the client's figure. I encourage clients to find a few silhouettes that work well and let me vary them as fashion changes, keeping the basic shapes the same. As I indicated in other chapters, understanding the client's figure and selecting enhancing designs minimizes fitting and saves time.

I am conscientious in directing my clients to the right shape for the garment, but I need **their** input for their fashion style. I also have a wonderful wardrobe consultant I can call on if I am ever in question. She will sit in on a consultation — an additional expense my clients are often willing to pay.

Instructing clients in color is fun, but I do not consider myself an expert. I encourage clients to have a color analysis; then we plan wardrobes around it. She will get more for her money if she follows a color and wardrobe plan. I work toward marrying every new garment into the wardrobe. I think making random pieces that don't work with others is a waste of time and money. I have a small wardrobe, but everything interacts. It has taken a lot of self-discipline, but it is worth it when everything fits together like a perfect puzzle.

CHAPTER 18

Be Organized to Work and Sew Fast

Scheduling My Life

I plan my days, weeks, months and even years in advance. I carry a calendar with me (a leather-bound 5″ × 7″ 3-ring binder with address and note sections) and we have THE CALENDAR in the family bathroom where I know everyone sees it each morning. Every personal and family event is on THE CALENDAR.

My Scheduling Rules:

1. I faithfully look at my calendar every night and morning.
2. I schedule at least one week in advance for everything. I think of my time like a dentist or doctor. Time is money.
3. I have standing appointments with clients that I pencil in a month in advance. These are regular clients who like to come the same day and time every week.
4. I write in pencil so I can easily erase. Life changes.
5. I put all of my son's basketball games and my daughter's tennis matches on my calendar. I want to be able to get away for what is important to my family.
6. I write down the phone number by every appointment. If I have to cancel or change I have the number handy.
7. Fabric sales dates are marked on my calendar. I keep a running list of client fabric and finding needs — buying on sale increases my profit. My list helps me maximize my shopping trips.
8. All school and family vacations are put on the calendar.
9. If I want free time to take a walk, I mark the time out on my calendar. If it is written down, I will do it.
10. In the address section I keep all personal and professional contacts, some filed by name and some by subject — whichever I will be more likely to remember.

My Basics of Time Management

♦ **Are you a morning or an evening person?** Recognize that and plan accordingly. Use high-gear time to do the top priority work (cutting) and low-gear time to do routine work (hemming).

♦ **Know when to stop working on a project.** I come to a point of diminishing returns, and have to stop working or the quality will go down. I make a daily list of things to accomplish in order of importance, including family responsibilities. I always over-plan, giving myself "stretch goals." I go for full completion of the list but don't always make it. Anything not completed goes to the next day's list.

♦ **Make use of your bits of time.** If you are waiting for a client, make phone calls, write notes, read a technical book, catch up on magazines, sew a seam on your personal sewing project.

♦ **Pool your family resources.** Ask family to do your errands. Tell them lovingly that you cannot work without their help. Be willing to write detailed lists of name brands and how much to spend. My kids are wise shoppers and research price and quality because they have been helping for so long.

♦ **Recognize, label, and eliminate irritants.** Much time is wasted when we lack control over our environment or our emotions. I hate being caught in traffic, so now I keep magazines and other materials with me at all times so I have something productive to do in case I have to wait.

♦ **Take charge of your telephone.** I installed a telephone answering machine. I can turn the volume up on my machine so that I can monitor my calls and can pick up the phone if it is an emergency. At the end of my work day I write down the messages and return calls while I do hand sewing or other "phone tasks." I have a portable phone that is convenient. I am told headsets are also useful.

I also have a separate phone line in my work area. When my children became teenagers, the competition for the phone was overwhelming! I realized the importance of the telephone in their social development so took that cue to install another line. I love it and should have done it long ago.

My Advice for Sane Sewing

♦ Invest in the best equipment you can afford.
♦ Teach yourself to concentrate under less than perfect conditions. Don't wait until everything is in order in the family and at home before you begin your work.

- Expand your thinking to work on more than one pattern, one piece of fabric, one client's project at a time. Think BIG! The worst thing that could happen is you could fail — the best lesson anyone can learn.
- Put everything you sew back in the bin or onto a hanger. Order creates an atmosphere of respect for your work.
- Change shoes halfway through the day for an energy boost.
- Lie down on the floor for five to ten minutes. Close your eyes, relax your mind, visualize a small creek and hear the sound of flowing water. It will help you relax and reduce stress.

Being Organized Helps Me Sew Faster

- Preshrink yards of elastic, linings, interfacings at one time. I do this while I cook dinner.
- Have wastebaskets everywhere in cutting and sewing areas. Hit them with scraps and threads to minimize cleanup.
- Have everything you need within reach. Be able to wheel your chair to different work spaces. Wasted motions cost money!
- Keep supplies and bobbins right next to the sewing machine.
- Group all thread by color. My daughter did this for me when she was ten years old and had nothing to do — I found it saves me time. I simply scan one area to find the right color. I return colors to their color family with thread ends hooked into the spool.
- Have a routine for cleanup. If done at night, it's ready for morning. I leave my work at night, but allow thirty minutes in the morning to cleanup. This gets my motor running and my head organized.

Efficient Cutting

- Set appointments for fittings which forces cutting. Pretreat the fabrics, collecting several projects to cut at one time.
- Plan your cut day for when it is quiet in your home. Allow enough time to think and plan the entire cut. Many changes may have been made on a design that require concentration. Do not leave the cutting layout half-finished. It is better not to start than not to allow time to complete the cutting.
- Have an iron nearby for pressing. Use a grid board for graining up fabric or use the edge of your cutting board to line up with the selvage. I tear or pull a thread at one end to start with a perfect cross grain.
- Turn off all electronic distractions (TV, stereo, etc.) when cutting.
- Have tape and pattern paper handy for alterations.

♦ Have every tool you will use hanging close at hand. I have a pegboard next to my cutting table. Or, you can wear an apron with pockets and slots for your scissors, rulers, pencils, etc.

♦ Have the table height right for you to minimize backaches.

♦ Use long blade shears for cutting — they make a longer cut.

♦ Keep all scraps of the garment until delivery time. Give the client her scraps and encourage her to save them. I can't tell you how handy it has been to do a repair or an after-completion design change because we saved the scraps.

♦ Set aside a shopping sample of each fabric for your client to use.

♦ Have a notebook handy with your work order in it. Write down **everything** you do. You may not remember when you make out the bill, so write it down now.

My Speed Sewing Tips

1. Read **Painless Sewing** by Palmer and Pletsch (see page 124). When I put their tips into action ten years ago, my production doubled.

2. Have a spare of every tool you use frequently.

3. Keep an inventory of the following on hand at all times: several types and weights of interfacing; many styles of shoulder pads; every color of thread; pins everywhere; zippers at least 9" long in every color.

4. Have machinery set to do specific things: piping, buttonholes; black thread; serger set for rolled hem. The more specialized your equipment is, the faster your production will be.

5. Wear snipping scissors and a tape measure around your neck.

6. If you have white thread on the machine, sew on every project that is white before changing thread.

7. Use all leftover bobbin threads for gathering. You will save time by **not** unwinding a bobbin only to rewind it.

8. Have at least 20 bobbins for each machine.

9. Turn your favorite lively music on when you want to sew fast.

10. Sew as many pieces of the garment as you can before pressing.

11. Baste by machine and learn to baste with glue.

12. Push your machine to sew as fast as it can stitch.

13. Sew an entire jacket lining (with sleeves already attached) into the jacket by machine.

14. Machine stitch any hem you possibly can.

15. Have more than one size and shape of pressing ham.

16. Consolidate hand sewing projects. Do four or five at a time while talking on the phone or watching TV with the family.

17. Make and cover shoulder pads in quantity.

CHAPTER 19

Good Equipment Makes Sewing Easier

Bare Bones Equipment to Begin

It doesn't take a lot of special equipment to get started in your home-based sewing business. Here is what I had and what I think is essential for you:

1. Sewing machine: After completing my first project for pay and deciding to make sewing my business, I traded in my sewing machine. My high school graduation gift of the 1960's just would not handle the new polyester fabrics of the 1970's. I chose a new, top-of-the-line, free-arm model. I borrowed $100 from our family budget for the down payment and made a deal with my sewing machine store, 90 days same as cash. It was a real risk for me as we had no family money to meet this debt. I wasn't sure I could make the $500 balance in just 90 days, but I made it all by myself! I was so proud!

You need these basic machine functions: quality straight stitch, zigzag, built-in buttonhole, overcast stitch and blind hem. Consider a good-quality, used machine if yours is tired and a new machine is out of your price range.

2. Free-arm table: My table was a sturdy model designed for sewing, with a flip-up surface that allowed access to the free-arm of my machine.

You need a sturdy sewing table that doesn't wobble and that is a comfortable height for sewing for long periods. If you have a free-arm machine, the free-arm table makes general sewing more comfortable.

3. Additional work table: I needed extra work space to support the weight of a long coat or long skirt at the end of my sewing machine table.

You need at least three feet of work surface beyond the sewing machine to hold bulky items.

4. Iron: I bought the best iron I could afford because I know how important good pressing is to a beautiful finished garment.

You need a "shot-of-steam" or "surge-of-steam" feature for bursts of steam in fusing and setting creases, lots of steam holes, Teflon® sole plate to prevent shine when top pressing, and as much metal in the sole plate as possible for extra weight that will make achieving a flat press easier. Do not purchase an iron that has the "automatic off" feature. You must leave your iron on for hours at a time to press as you sew.

5. Ironing board and cover: My family ironing board was covered with a silver Teflon coating, the latest thing in 1970. I didn't know then that the metallic cover intensified heat that caused overpressing. It also took me the longest time to figure out where the "grid marks" were coming from on fused areas of my garments. It was the metal pattern of the ironing board coming through a too-thin, worn-out pad.

You need a well-padded, absorbent (cotton or wool batting; polyester it not absorbent) ironing board surface with a clean, white 100% cotton cover.

6. Cutting surface: I started with the inexpensive cardboard type cutting board that is sold in fabric stores. I used it on the dining room table, the bed, or kitchen eating bar. I had two that I used together on the floor when I needed more cutting length.

You need a large flat space where you can easily cut without damaging the underneath surface. Waist height will be easier on your back.

7. Storage: I found storage containers with small drawers (generally used for nuts and bolts) in the discount store that were perfect for small notions. They were stacked under my extra table for easy access. For fabrics and interfacings I used cardboard storage chests that I hid under the beds.

You need a place to store small notions and fabrics as these items are part of your inventory and therefore part of your profit. Good organization and easy access are important features.

8. Full-length mirror: At the discount store I found an inexpensive mirror that I attached to the back of my bedroom door where I did my fittings.

You need a full-length, distortion-free mirror mounted in the private area where you will do fittings.

9. Extra light: Good room lighting is essential. In addition, a task light near your machine is a necessity, especially if you plan to sew at night. I used an old brass floor lamp that was not attractive but it did the job.

You need to acquire a floor lamp, clip-on lamp, or a table lamp that will add light directly to your sewing area without getting in your way.

10. Sewing chair: I used an old metal chair with a pillow on it; Pati Palmer used a little wooden stool without a back.

You need a chair that will give decent back support (unless you are in constant motion like Pati Palmer!) and a cushioned seat so you can sit for long periods. If you have back problems, a good chair should be one of your **first** major purchases. See page 46.

11. Miscellaneous items: Cutting shears, snipping scissors, tape measure, measuring gauge, good quality pins, press cloths, wastebaskets so you won't have to spend time cleaning.

I think I worked harder then than I do now, and produced so much less. My updated equipment helps me work faster and more efficiently.

My Beginning Equipment

♦ Sewing machine

♦ Ironing board
♦ Good home iron

♦ Cardboard cutting boards

♦ Free-arm sewing table
♦ Table to create "L"-shaped work space
♦ Floor lamp

♦ Full-length mirror

My Upgraded Equipment

♦ Three sewing machines, three sergers (see page 45)
♦ Cut and press board (see page 107)
♦ Sussman iron and a press (see page 106)
♦ Large padded cutting surface (see page 46)
♦ Customized sewing machine area
♦ Built-in "U"-shaped work space

♦ Good general room light from ceiling fluorescents plus fluorescent task lamps
♦ Three-way mirror

The Ultimate List of Tools

I have most of the following tools and recommend you add them to your studio also. All of them save time or help me produce a superior product. Buy them one by one as your profits allow, or ask for them for holiday or birthday gifts!

Sewing equipment:

♦ **Computerized sewing machine** - I like the versatility of home sewing machines. Top-of-the-line computerized machines offer many unique features that will make your sewing easier and faster. They often have a more powerful motor than less expensive machines for longer life and more piercing power through multiple layers. The disadvantage is that home sewing machines are not intended for production work and a warranty may be invalidated if it is discovered that the machine was used in business.

♦ **Power sewing machine** - A power machine stitches two to three times faster than a home machine, has a much more powerful motor, and lasts longer, but is limited in its functions. A power machine generally does one stitch only, so if you purchase a straight stitch you will also want a good home machine for zigzag, buttonholes, decorative stitching.

♦ **Extra sewing machines** - Keep all of your old sewing machines rather than trade them in. Keep them in good working order and you'll be surprised at how long they may last! I use different colors of thread on different machines so I can work on several projects at one time without changing threads. Use a spare machine when your primary one has to go to the "doctor," or take your extra machine with you to a sewing class. See page 45 for other ways I use additional machines in my sewing studio.

♦ **Sergers** - Begin with one basic serger, then add new machines as your volume and your profits allow. If you can, have one always set up for rolled edge and one for edge-finishing and decorative stitching. This saves time in machine adjustment. I think differential feed is an important feature to have in a new serger. See page 124 for other Palmer/Pletsch books on serging that give information on how to select and use a serger.

Pressing equipment:

◆ **Commercial iron** - I have the seven-pound Sussman Tailoring Iron which helps me produce better quality work. It also is a timesaver. It creates a tremendous amount of steam so it presses faster, has an accurate temperature gauge, and a Teflon® coating on the soleplate to eliminate shine. It can be used flat on an ironing board or table, or can steam at any angle should you need to press a garment while it is on a dress form. Water is automatically pumped through hoses attached to a tank, so there is no constant refilling. This has been an invaluable tool for me. No home iron available compares to the Sussman.

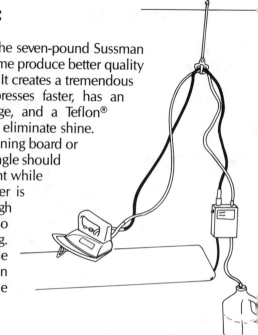

◆ **Press** - Similar to a dry cleaner's press, my smaller home version has a larger pressing surface which exerts 100 pounds of pressure when closed. This is an efficient way to fuse interfacings to fabric (I can fuse an entire jacket front at one time!) and to set creases and pleats. It is similar to the equipment used in the garment manufacturing industry. It has several temperature settings and an optional water sprayer. Mine is a dry press, but some models are steam presses. Presses are made by Elna, Viking (Husqvarna in Europe, Canada and Australia), and Singer. Look for them at your sewing machine stores.

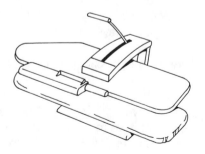

♦ **Padded pressing surface** — I gave up my ironing board when I discovered the versatile "cut 'n press board." The large surface makes it ideal for steam-shrinking fabrics and straightening and blocking off-grain fabrics. Use it also for fusing interfacings and pressing as you sew.

Palmer and Pletsch give the following insturctions for making this board in their book, **Pants for Any Body** (see page 124). Purchase a 32"×48" (⅓ of a 4'×8' sheet) piece of 5/8"-thick pressed board. Top it with a 1/2"-thick layer of old wool blankets or reprocessed, felted wool rug pad. (Do not use polyester batting — it is nonabsorbent.) Cover with heavy muslin and staple it to the back or tape with masking tape. Place it on a chest of drawers at elbow height next to your sewing machine

(To order the Palmer/Pletsch kit see page 123.)

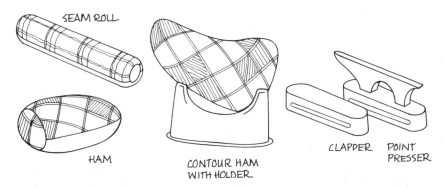

SEAM ROLL

HAM

CONTOUR HAM
WITH HOLDER

CLAPPER   POINT
PRESSER

Pressing aids:

♦ **Seam roll** — Place seams over this sausage-shaped tool when pressing them open to prevent the seam allowances from forming ridges that show to the right side.

♦ **Ham and ham holder** — Place the ham on the holder in the position desired to keep it from rolling around. Press curved areas over the ham to shape garments according to body contours. I prefer June Tailor hams, and have three of varying shapes and sizes.

♦ **Wooden tailor's clapper** (also available with an attached point presser that functions as a handle) — Flatten seams and bulky areas and crease pants and pleats during pressing. Steam the area well while it is on the seam roll, ham or padded pressing surface; apply the clapper for several seconds and repeat if necessary. The clapper forces steam into the fibers, then the wood absorbs the heat to cool the fabric. Only then will the fabric "stay put" in its newly-molded shape.

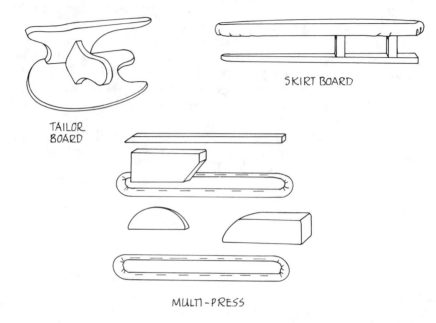

TAILOR BOARD

SKIRT BOARD

MULTI-PRESS

♦ **June Tailor tailor board** — Use this combination point presser and multi-curved press to press seams open in curved lapels and collars, rounded collars and cuffs. I like to use it with the optional padded cover for the top surface. Once you try it, you'll wonder how you lived without it!

♦ **June Tailor skirt board** — Resembling a giant sleeve board, this measures 36″ long and tapers from 9″ wide at one end to 6″ wide at the other. It is ideal for pressing inside skirts and pants, but I use it also for general pressing. It comes with a heavy cotton cover and a special velvet cover or "velva board."

♦ **Multi-Press** — This clever tool combines five specialty pressing pieces. It starts as a sleeve board with one side that detaches. That side can be replaced by a ham half or a long dowel to use like a seam roll or with a half-circle shape to use for pressing curves. I like this so much I have five of them: two for my studio and three for my students to use in my classes.

Cutting and marking tools:

♦ **Cutting table** — I now use a marvelous cutting table system that is a combination of a purchased table and the "cut 'n press board" method (see page 107). It is crucial that your cutting board be a comfortable height for you. My table can be raised or lowered depending on what I am cutting. I also wanted my board to be movable so I can walk completely around it and push it to any of the four sides to give me extra moving room.

   I can press on my board which is important for graining up fabric and for pressing wrinkles without the fabric falling off of the ironing board and stretching. The surface is also smooth enough for designing and pattern drafting, and the padded surface allows me to push pins into it which helps in drafting and in quick cutting. The large size also allows me to cut all widths of fabric easily.

♦ **Pattern weights** — I use weights for 75 percent of my cutting. Once you try them you will find they save a lot of time and increase your efficiency. They are available in many shapes and sizes; having an assortment is nice. Traditional tailor's weights have handles and little spikes in them to push into the fabric. Use small weights for detail pieces, larger ones for larger pattern pieces, and heavy weights for heavier fabrics. You may substitute small cans of food and kitchen items, but the right tool for the job is always the most efficient way. June Tailor has some attractive weights in the shape of common sewing tools.

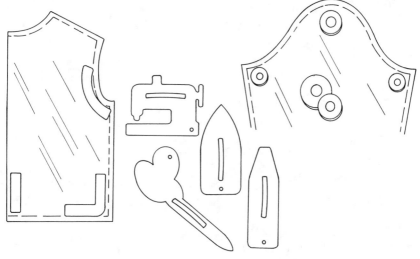

♦ **Fine Swiss pins** — I use these pins only for fine silks or fine detail pinning. I am very careful with them as they are fragile and hard to find. I have a separate pincushion just for these pins.

♦ **Magnetic pin holder** — I use at least four of these, both the dish and the wrist styles. I can toss pins toward a holder and it magnetically grabs them. It also saves me time when I must quickly pick up the spilled pin box. Try one at your desk for paper clips, too.

♦ **Scissors** — I have many different types of scissors and shears, both for paper patternmaking and for cutting fabric only. My family has learned that I have a piece of ribbon tied to every pair of scissors that they may use. No ribbon means the scissors may not touch anything but fabric. They respect my rule.

I wear small scissors tied on a pretty ribbon around my neck at all times when I am sewing. This way I never have to hunt for a scissors to snip or clip. Unfortunately, I am the absent-minded dressmaker and constantly embarrass my family by forgetting I am wearing my scissors as I run out to do my errands!

Buy the best quality you can afford in scissors and shears. They will reward you with a long life and easier and more efficient sewing. The brands are Henckels, Gingher, Wiss and Marks. I use the following shapes and sizes:

10" for silkies and efficient cutting.

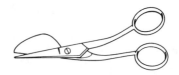

8" bent handled dressmaker shears for cutting. A sturdy lightweight is easy on the hands. Henckels is an excellent quality.

Applique scissors for beveling edges and trimming close to stitching.

Embroidery and needlework scissors (worn around the neck) for trimming, clipping, snipping.

I use pinking shears for notching curves and finishing seam allowances on some fabrics. I use a pair of 10½" heavy-duty shears (called "tailor's shears") for faster, smoother cutting on medium to heavy-weight fabrics. A tailor's supply store would carry them.

Good care is important for your scissors and shears. Have them professionally sharpened regularly.

♦ **Tailor's chalk or chalk wheel** — I like regular chalk, not the wax variety, as wax does not always come off the right side of a garment. Chalk must be sharp to be used properly; use a chalk sharpener or a paring knife to keep it to a sharp point.

The chalk wheel has replaced standard chalk for me. This nifty new item marks accurately with a perfect thin line of chalk made by a small wheel at the base of the marker. I have at least four so I can quickly lay my hands on one. I prefer white and light-colored chalk. Some colors are  so bright that I fear they will show through the fabric. Two brand names are "Chalkoner" and "EZ Chalk Wheel."

Hand sewing and basting aids:

♦ **Needles** — I like to have every size and type of sewing machine and hand sewing needle at my disposal. I am now able to purchase wholesale through the group-buying cooperative in our Custom Clothing Guild (see page 120).

♦ **Size A silk thread** - I use this for hand basting on lightweight silky fabrics. Because it is so fine, you can press over the thread and it will not leave a mark after it is removed. It is slippery so be sure to backstitch when basting, but do not use a knot.

♦ **Plain Tailor's Cotton Basting Thread** — This is my favorite for general basting. It is not slippery, but again do not use a knot.

◆ **Beeswax** — A coating of beeswax will strengthen thread and prevent knotting during hand sewing. I reel off about six yards of thread, folding one yard on top of the next. Then I run the thread through the beeswax, put it between two sheets of notebook paper and press the beeswax into the thread using a hot iron. Now I have enough thread ready to use for all of the hand sewing on one garment.

NOTE: After I run thread through beeswax, I tie each color into a loose bow, and then hang them in a specific spot until I am ready for hand sewing. Do this with the last bit of thread left on a bobbin or a spool!

◆ **Third-hand clamp** — Like the old-fashioned "sewing bird," this clamps onto the fabric to act like a third hand. I use it for hand sewing — hand rolling hems, finishing corners and fine details.

Measuring and pattern drafting tools:

NOTE: Many of these items are available in fabric shops, or office supply and art stores.

◆ **Long ruler** - I prefer metal and recommend two: 36″ and 45″. They can be used in drafting, to reach across the table to smooth out fabric, or as a long weight when graining up fabric.

◆ **Plastic see-through ruler** — The type with 1/8″ and 1/16″ grids will help your accuracy in altering and drafting patterns.

◆ **Hip-curve ruler**, fashion ruler, and French curve — All of these are necessary for shaping necklines, armholes, hiplines. The more choices you have in drafting and pattern altering aids the more proficient you will be.

FRENCH
CURVE

HIP CURVE
RULER

FASHION
RULER

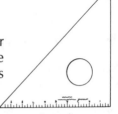

◆ **Triangle** — This is a plastic or metal piece with or without measurements. I use it for finding the true bias when cutting and for truing up 90° angles in drafting.

◆ **Measuring tape** — I have a metal-tipped plastic tape with inches on one side and centimeters and inches on the other. Be sure to compare yours to a metal ruler as tape measures can be inaccurate.

◆ **Compass** — This tool is used for drawing circles and arcs in drafting. I also use it to mark seamlines on patterns that do not have them and to add seam allowances to patterns I have drafted or altered. I have found the higher quality compass produces a better quality product for me.

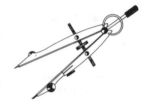

◆ **Push pins** — I use these for anchoring patterns so I can pivot the paper in pattern drafting.

◆ **1/2" Scotch Brand Magic Transparent Tape** — Buy a desk dispenser (it's easier to use) and tape in quantity for patternmaking, altering patterns, and sewing.

Additional invaluable timesavers:

The following items are so important to me that I have three or four of each. I don't want to waste time searching for a $1.00 gadget when having multiples will save me time. I place them at different machines, my cutting area, and the pressing area.

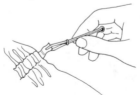

◆ **Point turner** — to turn points right side out without poking through fabric. I prefer bamboo to plastic.

◆ **Bodkin** — "pinch and pull" type for threading elastic through a casing.

◆ **Long tweezer** — for serger threading, pulling out threads, removing jammed threads and pins from machines.

♦ **Awl** — to rip out stitching. It is safer than a seam ripper as it won't cut fabric.

♦ **Needle-nose pliers** — to remove tough pins, pull hand needles through tough fabrics, tighten machine parts, grip things while turning right side out.

♦ **Measuring gauge** — one at every cutting, sewing and pressing area to measure seam allowances, just everything!

♦ **Small screw driver** — for machine use.

♦ **"Snag-Be-Gone"** — repair snags in any fabric.

♦ **Thimble** — for all hand sewing.

♦ **Bias tape maker** — this clever tool folds bias strips into perfect bias tape.

BIAS TAPE MAKER— TWO VIEWS

The balance of my list is equally important but I don't have multiples due to less frequent use or much higher price!

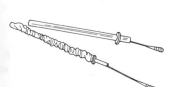

♦ **"Fasturn" tube turner** — turns all tubing from thin loops to wide belts.

♦ **Buttonhole cutter** — neatly slices open machine buttonholes.

♦ **Button elevator** — raises sew-through buttons so a shank is created easily.

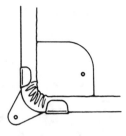

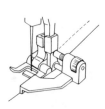

♦ **Pocket former template** — for pressing fabric around a curved metal template to create perfect pocket corners.

♦ **Topstitching foot** — a presser foot that aids in easy, even topstitching.

♦ **Pintuck foot** — for double-needle pintucking, to add special custom touches to collars, pockets, etc.

114

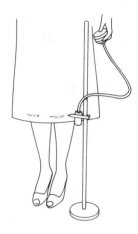

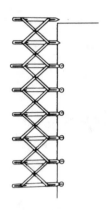

♦ **Hem marker** — uses chalk for accurate and easy marking of your own or client's hems.

♦ **Simflex gauge** — expandable measuring device that makes button and buttonhole spacing a snap.

♦ **Dress form** — custom-made plaster forms (see page 120) are my preference.

♦ **Fabric finish** — spray on during final pressing to flatten fabric and give a firm and crisp press.

♦ **Fluorescent task lights** — clamp onto edge of table, with movable arm; available with attached magnifying glass for extremely close work.

♦ **Spot remover** — I use hair spray to remove ink stains, "Energine" for other spots, and let the dry cleaner do the tough ones. Test first!

♦ **Fusible web** — buy by the yard and cut your own strips.

♦ **Smooth tracing wheel** — use with tracing paper to mark everything marked during cutting. (Use chalk for marking during fitting.)

♦ **Quilting guide** — attaches to machine above presser foot, or to the foot itself, to gauge seam allowance widths.

I would want and need all of these tools as a home-sewer, but because I **need** them for my work as a dressmaker, I can deduct them for tax purposes as a business expense. Just one more advantage!

CHAPTER 20

Expanding Your Business

Hiring Help

When your business grows to the point that it takes two months or longer to move a project through your studio, it is time to find some help. Develop a network of people to contract out some of your work. Hiring help can increase your profits, but if your original goal was to simplify your life and keep your overhead low, hiring employees or subcontractors may create more problems than profits.

It is often difficult to find someone to do the quality work that you require. The ideal person is a skilled home-sewer who would love a part-time job but doesn't want to have her own sewing business. I am lucky to have two excellent subcontractors — one does dressmaking (including time-consuming details such as pleats and tucks) and one does my pant sewing (she cuts from a corrected pattern, sews details and bastes the pants together for the first fitting). They are well-trained in my style of sewing.

I put down on paper exactly what they are to do and set deadlines. We have established the piece work rate or an hourly rate. Their hourly rate is much lower than mine because they work slowly. We have an understanding that I will reward good work and pay on time and they will correct unsatisfactory work.

Moving to a Retail Space

Most dressmakers eventually wonder what it would be like to move all of the confusion to a retail space. I did just that. It was an exciting adventure and I learned a lot — primarily that I could not leave and go home when I wanted to. I had to keep regular hours, and overhead expenses ate my hard-earned money. I finally moved my business back home to increase my wages and to get back in touch with my family. I can't tell you how happy I was to be back home! I like the flexibility and greater profits of working from home. Can you tell I do not recommend a venture into retail space? If you want to live there instead of at home, be my guest!

CHAPTER 21

A Home-Based Business and the Family

Keeping the Family Happy

The most frequently asked question when I speak on **Sewing As a Business** is, "How do you integrate a business in the home with family — without problems?" It is not without difficulty, but try to work smarter, be more self-disciplined, have better organizational skills and more patience. I made my choice with the birth of my first child — my business would grow as my children grew, and it has. The pace I keep today no longer allows the amount of time I spent with my children when they were small.

I created a work plan that fits into my family life. I work hard all day so that I can be with my family in the evening. I save paperwork, hand sewing, planning and reading for evenings so I can be in the same room with them and still be productive. I go to bed when the family is ready, but I may rise at 4:30am to get all of my work done.

I have a patient and forgiving husband. The security of his job gave me the opportunity to raise our children and evolve into a career woman. In the beginning we created a lot of of unnecessary confusion for each other, but I was determined that the family and the business would both thrive.

A more loving atmosphere emerged ten years ago because we learned better communication skills. We discovered that I am an expressive person and need room and lots of activity, while Mike is more of an introvert who likes to be alone. We now see those characteristics as assets instead of threats. We have worked out cooperative arrangements for child rearing, decision-making, household chores and shopping. We work to uplift and compliment each other. **Cooperation** and **respect** are the best words I can give for success in mixing family and work under the same roof.

Keeping Myself Sane

For me to thrive it is important to me to stay on an exercise program. The benefits are so noticeable. While working I am confined to a chair or standing in one place for long periods of time. Exercise relieves my body of the resulting stress and pain. I like to walk two miles three times a week and often walk with family. I get quality time with them as well as good exercise. I do calisthenics by video that strengthen my back and improve my posture. A home plan is best for me; I would never get in the car to go to a club.

Keeping My House Tidy

Clients are guests in your living room if you don't have a separate work space. I want to make the best impression so I keep my studio as tidy as I can. When I was sewing in the family room, we devised a great system to keep the house in order. It was called "THE BOX." At bedtime, anything left out of place (toys or clothing belonging to the children or us) was picked up and placed into THE BOX for a penalty period of seven days. Today, even with teenagers, we have a tidy house. It taught me to put my shoes away — I once had to go without my best pair for seven days!

Keeping My Family Clothed

I am a dressmaker because I love to create beautiful clothing — and to earn money doing it. I sew what my family cannot afford to buy, or what I love to sew. I will make a $450 Ultrasuede® blazer for my husband or a $250 wool coat for my daughter. These are the types of things I have a passion to create. I do not have a passion to sew T-shirts, and those I can afford to buy ready-made. Think this over if you feel guilty because you are not sewing all of your family's clothing while you are sewing for others for profit.

I taught my son and daughter how to evaluate what I will make and what they can buy. They do all of their own shopping for fabric and ready-to-wear. I spent several years training them to be smart shoppers. We base the decision on quality of fabric, longevity of design, price, and how many hours I have to sew to achieve the same look. If it is a fad style I will probably not sew it and definitely not if the retail price is under $35.

The premise that women sew to clothe their families for less is no longer true. Now we sew to express our creativity and to increase the quality of our families' clothing.

CHAPTER 22

My Best Wishes to You

I hope you have enjoyed my story and have learned from it. Dressmaking has been a rewarding career for me and I love to promote this way of life. Today I can see the rewards of my work to combine the roles of homemaker and career woman in the same space. My children at ages 16 and 17 have developed and matured. They are working partners with me in both my business and home. My husband and I are closer than I dreamed

possible. I am receiving financial rewards for the business knowledge, technical skill and experience I have developed in my field. I wish this same success to you.

Important Resources

Kathleen Spike
1880 S.W. Heiney Road
Gresham, OR 97080
(503) 665-6505

Feel free to write or call. I charge a consulting fee of $25 per hour. Send a check requesting consultation and I will phone you back, collect.

Custom Clothing Guild of Oregon
P.O. Box 18163
Portland, OR 97218

Write for an information packet on how to start your own local guild.

Success Stories People:

Jeanne Scolaro Brown
Designer Sample Maker
Oregon
(503) 626-8816

Delores Dianne Kelley
Custom Interior Sewing
Portland, Oregon
(503) 249-2882

Ann Franzen
Garment Manufacturer
3020 S.E. 17th
Gresham, OR 97080
(503) 667-8221

Paula Marineau
Wearable Art Designer
4120 S.W. 83rd
Portland, OR 97225
(503) 292-5677

Bonnie Sponsel
Custom plaster dress forms
1630 May Street N.E.
Keizer, Oregon 97303
(503) 393-0205

Beth Duncan
State Clothing Specialist
Mississippi Cooperative Extension
Service, P.O. Box 5446
Mississippi State, MS 39762
(601) 325-3081

Small Business Administration (SBA)
Look in your local phone directory under U.S. Government.

Service Corps of Retired Executives (SCORE)
Call or visit your nearest Small Business Administration office to reach this division of SBA. SCORE provides management counseling to small businesses, community organizations and not-for-profit groups.

Cooperative Extension Service
Look in your local phone directory under your county services listing for "Extension Service." They will provide you with the booklet "Sewing for Profit," state license and permit requirements, and other business, sewing and textile-related information.

Bibliography

Home-Based Business Resources

Price It Right, Claire Shaeffer, La Mode Illustree, P.O. Box 157, Palm Springs, CA 92263, 1984

Sewing as a Home Business, Mary Roehr, P.O. Box 20898, Tallahassee, FL 32316-0898, 1984

Women Working Home, Marion Behr and Wendy Lazar, Rodale Press, Inc., 1983

Working from Home, Paul and Sarah Edwards, Houghton Mifflin Co., 1985

Psychology and Communications Resources

How to Survive Being Alive, Dr. Donald L. Dudley and Elton Welke, Signet New American Library, 1977

Pulling Your Own Strings, Wayne W. Dyer, Avon, 1979

Skills for Success, Adele Scheele, Ph.D., Ballantine Books, 1979

Stress, Sanity and Survival, Robert L. Woolfolk, Ph.D. and Frank C. Richardson, Signet New American Library, 1978

Your Erroneous Zones, Wayne W. Dyer, Funk and Wagnalls, 1969

History of Fashion Resources

Elsa Schiaparelli: Empress of Paris Fashion, Palmer White, Rizzoli, 1986

Fabulous Fashion, 1907-1967, The Metropolitan Museum of Art, International Cultural Corporation of Australia Limited

Wardrobe, Color and Figure Analysis Resources

Color Me Beautiful, Carole Jackson, Ballantine Books, 1980

Color Wonderful, Joanne Nickolson and Judy Lewis Crum, with Jacqueline Thompson, Bantam Books, 1986

Complete Bonnie August Dress Thin System, Bonnie August, Rawson Wade Publishers Inc., 1981

Fashion and Color, Kojiro Kumagai, Graphic-sha Publishing Co., Ltd., 1985

The Fashion Coloring Book, Sharon Lee Tate and Mona Shafer Edwards, Harper & Row, 1984

It's You!, Emily Cho, Villard Books, 1986

Short Chic, Allison Kyle Leopold and Anne Marie Cloutier, Bantam, 1983

You Are What You Make Yourself, Ann Vaughn and Madeline Pober, Seaview Books, 1980

Designing and Drafting Resources

The Art of Fashion Draping, Connie Amaden Crawford, Fairchild Publications, 1989

Decorative Dressmaking, Sue Thompson, Rodale Press, 1985

Design and Sew It Yourself, Lois Ericson and Diane Ericson Frode, P.O. Box 1680, Tahoe City, CA 95730, 1983

Fabrics...Reconstructed, Lois Ericson, P.O. Box 1680, Tahoe City, CA 95730, 1985

Fashion Sketchbook, Bina Abling, Fairchild Publications, 1988

How to Make Sewing Patterns, Donald W. McCunn, Design Enterprises of SF, P.O. Box 27677, San Francisco, CA 94127, 1977

Master Designer System, Dept. R-35, 343 South Dearborn Street, Chicago, IL 60604, 1985

Personal Patterns by Jinni, Virginia Nastiuk (author and publisher), 1986

Professional Patternmaking for Designers, Jack Wandford, 1984

Sewing Technique Books and Videos

Classic Tailoring Techniques, Roberta Cabrera and Patricia Flaherty Meyers, Fairchild Publications, 1986

Fast Fashion Jeans for Family Fun, Roberta Harlan and Kathleen Spike, 1880 S.W. Heiney Road, Gresham, OR 97080

How to Sew Leather, Suede and Fur, Phyllis W. Schwebke and Margaret B. Krohn, Collier Macmillan, 1966, 1970

Men's Custom Tailored Pants, Stanley Hostek, Tailor-Craft, 4003 West Armour Street, Seattle, WA 98199, 1970

Palmer/Pletsch books and videos (see page 124), including *Sewing to Success* video featuring Kathleen Spike, 1989

Fashion and Sewing Periodicals

McCall's Patterns, The McCall Pattern Company, P.O. Box 3325, Manhattan, KS 66502-9917

Sew It Seams, P.O. Box 2698, Kirkland, WA 98083

Sew News, PJS Publications, Inc., P.O. Box 1790, Peoria, IL 61656

Threads, The Taunton Press, P.O. Box 355, Newton, CT 06470

Vogue Patterns, P.O. Box 751, Altoona, PA 16003

"W" 1-800-344-2211

Book Sources

Fairchild Books, 7 E. 12th Street, NY, NY 10003 (ask for free catalog of fashion and design books)

Gossamer Publishing, P.O. Box 84963, Seattle, WA 98124 (catalog of hundreds of books, magazines and videos)

R.L. Shep, Box C-20, Lopes Island, WA 98261 (publishers and booksellers)

Wooden Porch Books, Rt. 1, Box 262, Middlebourne, WV 26149

Tailoring Supplies

Oregon Tailor Supply, 2123-A S.E. Division Street, Portland, OR 97202

Palmer/Pletsch Associates (write to address on next page) for "cut 'n press" board padding kit.

Related Items from Palmer/Pletsch

Sew to Success
Video (45 min.)
$29.95

Bulletin:
Trends in
Sewing Room
Design (8-page)
$3.95

More Products from Palmer/Pletsch

Look for these Palmer/Pletsch easy-to-use, information-filled sewing books and videos in local fabric stores, or contact us for ordering information.

☐ **The Serger Idea Book—A Collection of Inspiring Ideas from Palmer/Pletsch,** Color photos and how-to's on inspiring and fashionable ideas from the Extraordinary to the Practical. *8½×11, 160 pgs., $18.95*

Books available spiral bound— add $3.00 for large books, $2.00 for small.

☐ **Creative Serging for the Home and Other Quick Decorating Ideas,** by *Lynette Ranney Black and Linda Wisner.* Color photos and how-to's to help you transform your home into the place you want it to be. *8½×11, 160 pgs., $18.95*

☐ **Sewing Ultrasuede Brand Products** by *Marta Alto, Pati Palmer and Barbara Weiland.* Fashion photo section, plus the newest techniques to master these luxurious fabrics. *8½×11, 128 pgs., $16.95*

☐ **Sewing With Sergers—The Complete Handbook for Overlock Sewing,** *by Pati Palmer and Gail Brown.* Learn easy threading tips, stitch types, rolled edging and flatlocking on your serger. *128 pgs., Revised Edition $8.95*

☐ **Creative Serging—The Complete Handbook for Decorative Overlock Sewing,** by *Pati Palmer, Gail Brown and Sue Green.* In-depth information and creative uses of your serger. *128 pgs., $6.95*

☐ **Creative Serging Illustrated,** Same as Creative Serging PLUS color photography. *160 pgs., $14.95 (Not available in spiral)*

☐ **Sew to Success!—How to Make Money in a Home-Based Sewing Business,** by *Kathleen Spike.* Learn how to establish your market, set policies and procedures, price your talents and more! *128 pgs., $10.95*

☐ **Mother Pletsch's Painless Sewing,** *Revised Edition, by Pati Palmer and Susan Pletsch.* The most uncomplicated sewing book of the century! Filled with sewing tips on how to sew FAST! *128 pgs., $6.95*

☐ **Sensational Silk—A Handbook for Sewing Silk and Silk-like Fabrics,** by *Gail Brown.* Complete guide for sewing with silkies from selection to perfection in sewing. *128 pgs., $6.95*

☐ **Easy, Easier, Easiest Tailoring,** *Revised Edition, by Pati Palmer and Susan Pletsch.* Learn 4 different tailoring methods, easy fit tips, and timesaving machine lining. *128 pgs., $6.95*

☐ **Pants For Any Body,** *Revised Edition, by Pati Palmer and Susan Pletsch.* Learn to fit pants with clear step-by-step problem and solution illustrations. *128 pgs., $6.95*

☐ **Clothes Sense—Straight Talk About Wardrobe Planning,** by *Barbara Weiland and Leslie Wood.* Learn to define your personal style and when to sew or buy. *128 pgs., $6.95*

☐ **Sew a Beautiful Wedding,** by *Gail Brown and Karen Dillon.* Bridal how-to's on choosing the most flattering style to sewing with specialty fabrics. *128 pgs., $6.95*

☐ **Couture Sewing,** by *Roberta Carr.* Coming March 1992.

VIDEOS— *$29.95 each* (VHS only)
☐ **Sewing the Time Saving Way** *(45 min.)*
☐ **Sewing to Success** *(45 min.)*
☐ **Sewing With Sergers — Basics** *(1 hr.)*
☐ **Sewing With Sergers — Advanced** *(1 hr.)*
☐ **Creative Serging** *(1 hr.)*
☐ **Creative Serging II** *(1 hr.)*
☐ **Sewing with Ultrasuede** *(1 hr.)*

We also publish a series of **Trends Bulletins,** and carry hard-to-find and unique threads (Decor 6 Rayon, Woolly Nylon, Candlelight metallic threads—order our color cards for $2), notions, and **Henckels sewing scissors.** If not available at a store near you, write for more information.

Palmer Pletsch Associates
P.O. Box 12046
Portland, OR 97212
(503) 274-0687

International orders please pay in U.S. funds or with Visa or MasterCard. Shipping and handling: ($1–13.99) $1.75; ($14–24) $2.00; ($25–29.99) $3.00; ($50+) $4.00. Please allow 4–6 weeks for delivery.

"Camera-Ready" Forms

Take these forms to your printer. Enlarge them to full size and have printer or typesetter put your business information over mine.

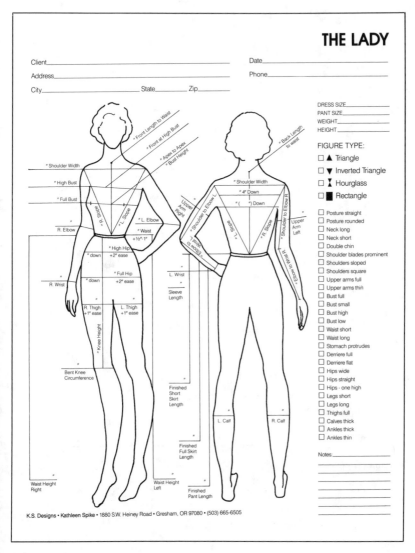

THE LADY

Client_____ Date_____

Address_____ Phone_____

City_____ State_____ Zip_____

DRESS SIZE_____
PANT SIZE_____
WEIGHT_____
HEIGHT_____

FIGURE TYPE:

☐ ▲ Triangle
☐ ▼ Inverted Triangle
☐ ⅄ Hourglass
☐ ■ Rectangle

☐ Posture straight
☐ Posture rounded
☐ Neck long
☐ Neck short
☐ Double chin
☐ Shoulder blades prominent
☐ Shoulders sloped
☐ Shoulders square
☐ Upper arms full
☐ Upper arms thin
☐ Bust full
☐ Bust small
☐ Bust high
☐ Bust low
☐ Waist short
☐ Waist long
☐ Stomach protrudes
☐ Derriere full
☐ Derriere flat
☐ Hips wide
☐ Hips straight
☐ Hips - one high
☐ Legs short
☐ Legs long
☐ Thighs full
☐ Calves thick
☐ Ankles thick
☐ Ankles thin

Notes:_____
_____
_____
_____
_____
_____
_____

K.S. Designs • Kathleen Spike • 1880 S.W. Heiney Road • Gresham, OR 97080 • (503) 665-6505

Enlarge 200% to print 8½ ×11

125

WORK AGREEMENT

KS

for
KATHLEEN SPIKE

Date In_____

Date Needed_____

Date Finished_____

Amt. Yardage Received_____
Checked for Flaws_____
Fiber Content_____
Dry Clean_____ Wash_____

Notions Received: _____
_____
_____
_____

Findings Purchased:
_____ $_____
_____ _____
_____ _____
_____ _____
_____ _____
_____ _____
_____ _____
Total $_____

Estimated Labor Charge $_____
Actual Recorded Time _____
Final Costs:
_____ _____
_____ _____
_____ _____
_____ _____
Total $_____

Deposit Received $_____
Balance due upon completion of project.

Client Name_____ Date_____
Address_____
City_____ State_____ Zip_____
Phone_____

PROJECT_____ Pattern #_____
_____ Pattern #_____
CONSTRUCTION & SKETCHES

Client Signature_____ Date_____

KS Designs Signature_____

Design · Dressmaking · Instruction
1880 S.W. Heiney Road
Gresham, OR 97080
(503) 665-6505

Enlarge 200% to print 8½ × 11

KS

for
KATHLEEN SPIKE

YOUR COMMENTS, PLEASE

Date_____

Please help me keep you a satisfied customer. Complete this evaluation and return it to me so I can serve you better another time.

PROJECT_____

FOR_____

	Very Satisfactory	Acceptable	Unsatisfactory
GENERAL APPEARANCE Comments:			
FIT Comments:			
DETAILS Comments:			
Other Comments:			

Thank you for your cooperation.

_____
KS Designs

Design · Dressmaking · Instruction
1880 S.W. Heiney Road
Gresham, OR 97080
(503) 665-6505

Enlarge 200% to print 8½×11

This form was adapted from materials prepared by clothing specialists with the Texas Agricultural Extension Service.

KS

INVOICE

for
**KATHLEEN
SPIKE**

date _____

to _____

_____

_____

Design • Dressmaking • Instruction
1880 S.E. Heiney Road
Gresham, OR 97080
(503) 665-6505

*Enlarge 130% to 5½×8½.
We suggest printing on 3-part NCR paper.*